gel

tter

Aaron Spiegel

Synagogues Matter

Hadassa Word Press

Impressum / Imprint

Bibliografische Information der Deutschen Nationalbibliothek: Die Deutsche Nationalbibliothek verzeichnet diese Publikation in der Deutschen Nationalbibliografie; detaillierte bibliografische Daten sind im Internet über http://dnb.d-nb.de abrufbar.
Alle in diesem Buch genannten Marken und Produktnamen unterliegen warenzeichen-, marken- oder patentrechtlichem Schutz bzw. sind Warenzeichen oder eingetragene Warenzeichen der jeweiligen Inhaber. Die Wiedergabe von Marken, Produktnamen, Gebrauchsnamen, Handelsnamen, Warenbezeichnungen u.s.w. in diesem Werk berechtigt auch ohne besondere Kennzeichnung nicht zu der Annahme, dass solche Namen im Sinne der Warenzeichen- und Markenschutzgesetzgebung als frei zu betrachten wären und daher von jedermann benutzt werden dürften.

Bibliographic information published by the Deutsche Nationalbibliothek: The Deutsche Nationalbibliothek lists this publication in the Deutsche Nationalbibliografie; detailed bibliographic data are available in the Internet at http://dnb.d-nb.de.
Any brand names and product names mentioned in this book are subject to trademark, brand or patent protection and are trademarks or registered trademarks of their respective holders. The use of brand names, product names, common names, trade names, product descriptions etc. even without a particular marking in this work is in no way to be construed to mean that such names may be regarded as unrestricted in respect of trademark and brand protection legislation and could thus be used by anyone.

Coverbild / Cover image: www.ingimage.com

Verlag / Publisher:
Hadassa Word Press
ist ein Imprint der / is a trademark of
OmniScriptum GmbH & Co. KG
Bahnhofstraße 28, 66111 Saarbrücken, Deutschland / Germany
Email: info@hadassa-wp.com

Herstellung: siehe letzte Seite /
Printed at: see last page
ISBN: 978-3-639-79448-9

ACKNOWLEDGEMENTS

Synagogues matter. If I convey nothing else in this book, it is my belief that the most important institution in American Jewish life is the synagogue. I believe that synagogues will continue to be the most important institution in American Jewish life. However, their success or failure is directly proportional to the viability of American Judaism. That said, synagogues must change, some radically. They must reflect contemporary American life, while at the same time informing American Judaism. I did not come to these conclusions on my own, therefore I must recognize those whose influence I treasure.

For the last fifteen-plus years, my colleagues at the Center for Congregations have taught me that congregations are immeasurably important in all areas of society. They have also taught me that synagogues are light years behind churches in resources for professionalizing congregations and ensuring that they remain viable and significant.

My years with Synagogue 3000 were life changing, and allowed me to test some of the lessons learned working with churches on synagogues. This time also confirmed for me that synagogues are capable of radical change if given the resources, training, and encouragement. My friends and colleagues Dr. Ron Wolfson, Dr. Steven Cohen, Rabbi Jessica Zimmerman, and Rabbi Lawrence Hoffman were my partners in reinventing the status quo and, in great Jewish form, often through debate and downright argument – always in love and respect – for the benefit of the Jewish people.

I want to make special mention of my mentor, teacher, and dear of friend, Larry Hoffman. From our first meeting, it was clear that we were of like minds and he was a champion of congregations and is always my partner in advocating for synagogues.

Sarah Brown is my editor cum laude. Starting with this project as my doctoral dissertation she has read this work more than anyone (probably including me) and helped me express myself clearly and cogently.

Finally, my wife Kelly who puts up with my impatience with the pace of change in the synagogue world. If we had saints, she would certainly be eligible. And, my children – Hannah, Elijah, and Gabriel, for whom I hope to help create a Judaism that is part of their lives. Their expression of Jewishness is their own and my hope is that they, as well as other young people, find the intellectual stimulation, reward, beauty, grace, and blessing that is Judaism.

CONTENTS

THE PROBLEM

Jewish identity in America can no longer rely on culture or ethnicity to sustain it, as it has in previous generations. Affiliation rates in synagogues are on a steady decline, and American Jews, particularly younger Jews, have lost the historic value of affiliation. The American Jewish community is more intimate and comfortable with the non-Jewish world than ever in history[1]. This intimacy has enabled Jews to thrive as never before. This comfort is countered by a downside – with acceptance by its non-Jewish neighbors comes new levels of acculturation – Jews want to be like their non-Jewish contemporaries. The American Jewish community wrestles with the fine line between acculturation and distinctive Jewishness. This then leads to the question, why be Jewish? Past motivations, including ethnic identifications, no longer sustain the Jewish community.[2] Without these ethnic and even cultural distinctions, the Jewish community is seeking something else that creates uniqueness and connectedness.

It is my contention that something else is needed to reclaim the collective wisdom of lived theology (Jewishness) as it pertains to synagogues. Formal, propositional theology is problematic for Judaism. For most of its history, it is impossible for Judaism to speak of its relationship with God devoid of Jewish practice (at least since the rabbinic period, 1st to 3rd Century A.C.E.). Jews often talk about Judaism as lived theology; it is through one's works and deeds that one comes to an understanding of God's relation to the world. For centuries, this theory was reasonable and sufficient. Only the "thinkers" questioned the nature of this theory. The *baalei batim* (literally "masters of the home") or general members of the community either took this God-World relationship for granted or simply did not consider it an important aspect of their Judaism. As Jews become more acculturated, they become more reflective about God's relationship to them and their world, and it is this very reflective relationship that I want to explore, especially as it relates to synagogues.

---

[1]   Ari Kelman and Eliana Schonberg, *Legwork, Framework, Artwork: Engaging the Next Generation of Jews* (Colorado: The Rose Community Foundation, 2008), 10-11.
[2]   Rabbi Lawrence Hoffman, *ReThinking Synagogues: A New Vocabulary for Congregational Life* (Woodstock, Vermont: Jewish Lights, 2006), 6.

1

This book seeks to illustrate how committed synagogue members account for their synagogue involvement, and how it contributes to their Jewishness. Using an interview method that uncovers tacit knowledge, I sought to uncover knowledge that is not readily conscious, looking to discover that collective wisdom of communal commitment that is part of the collective psyche of committed synagogue members. Moreover, it is this tacit, collective wisdom that might inform a new language that is full of transcendent meaning, allowing committed synagogue members to communicate that value to disaffected and unaffiliated Jews.

CONTEXTUAL CONDITIONS

My contention is that the synagogue is the central institution for Jewish community. Those who affiliate with synagogues have an implicit (as well as the obvious explicit) connection to Judaism that those who do not affiliate lack. However, this connection is buried and difficult to identify. Synagogues still matter, and if these implicit connections can be surfaced, a new language of value may surface. This could become an invaluable tool for synagogues.

The context is really the question, "why be Jewish?" By extension, why be part of a synagogue and the Jewish community? Since Judaism, unlike other faiths like Christianity and Islam, has no creed or doctrine, defining Jewishness (other than birthright) is difficult for some Jews. Does Jewish identity form from relationship to the community, or does community relationship enhance some tacit Jewishness that already exists?

Another complicating factor is that synagogues cannot measure viability as churches who, for the most part, gauge health by worship attendance. Synagogue 3000's recent FACT survey reported "Saturday morning services in Conservative synagogues drew an average of 24 worshipers for every 100 member families. Friday evening services at Reform temples drew an average of 17 worshipers for every 100 families."[3] So, a 1000 family synagogue nets an average of 170 worshippers for weekly Shabbat services. Put simply, Jews do not go to synagogue for worship. The reasons are varied from Judaism's focus on the home to lackluster worship experience.

Judaism lacks (and I propose needs) an ecclesiology of synagogue, or as Larry Hoffman puts it, 'people-ology'[4] to replace religious ethnicity. It is not that the institution of the synagogue is the be all/end all place, as much as the fact that no other institution in American Jewish life is better positioned to present Judaism in a valid, relevant, lived faith. I want to provide a narrative to those suspicious of the organized Jewish community, and a narrative for synagogues to be able to

---

[3] "Reform and Conservative Congregations: Different Strengths, Different Challenges," S3K Report (March 2012), 2.
[4] L. Hoffman, personal communication, 11 May 2007.

express a compelling, rational promotion of the importance of the synagogue to those who feel there is little value to synagogue membership.

This book then, seeks to 1) show patterns of Jewish experience that reflect the importance of the synagogue, 2) provide a narrative to those suspicious of traditional Jewish community, and 3) provide a narrative for synagogues to promote their importance.

This project developed from my work with Synagogue 3000 and as a resource consultant for the Indianapolis Center for Congregations (ICC). My work with ICC over the last fifteen years has been primarily with churches and the field of congregational redevelopment. Much of the work of the church community over the last twenty years is unknown in the synagogue community. Moreover, much of the church redevelopment work that is known to the synagogue community is either discounted or deemed irrelevant because of language and context. I posit that much of this work is far from irrelevant. It merely needs translation and contextualizing in order to work appropriately for synagogues.

The primary sustaining force behind continued synagogue affiliation has been ethnic identity. Following Eisenhower's charge that all Americans join a congregation in the early 1950's, Jews joined synagogues; Christians joined churches. While Christians brought to church theological doctrine as the glue that held them together, Jews brought ethnicity. Jews joined synagogues bringing what they had, a sense of ethnic identity fostered by parents and grandparents who either had personal or second-hand experience of the 'old country.' American Judaism is no longer sustained by this ethnic identity. We are now in the second, perhaps third generation of Jews who have no direct connection to relatives who were born outside of America.

Hoffman defines ethnicity as,

"... a nostalgic yearning for Jewish folkways that once sustained us as a people apart, but can no longer do so - not, at least, without anti-Semitism to drive it. Ethnicity in this sense is doing what we think Jews have always done, whether they are really what Jews have always done or not, and whether or not they are even authentically Jewish; and doing them by social habit, just because we have grown up with them and feel good doing them. Jewish ethnicity is 'doing what comes naturally,' but with no transcendent purpose.[5]

---

[5]   Rabbi Lawrence Hoffman, *ReThinking Synagogues: A New Vocabulary for Congregational Life* (Woodstock, Vermont: Jewish Lights, 2006), 5.

To distinguish ethnicity from culture, Hoffman writes,

"By Jewish culture, I mean the totality of wisdom, practices, folkways and so forth that constitute what we choose to remember of Jewish experience. That experience is simply too massive for anyone to remember it all, so every generation selects part of it (reinterpreting it as necessary), and leaves the rest behind. Leaving behind does not mean losing it forever, however. The parts of Jewish culture that do not get selected in any given generation remain in the cultural reservoir, as it were, to be recovered some day by others."[6]

He contends that culture remains viable and important to Judaism because of, " … the remarkable fact that Judaism demands study, and not just study of what is relevant, but study of everything Jewish."[7]

To state this another way, ethnicity does not sustain the American Jewish community because it is grounded in 'feel-good' habits that have no transcendent purpose. In contrast, culture is based on the dynamic nature of Judaism and its ability to stay current, vibrant, and congruent with general culture. However, as Hoffman points out, culture takes study. Without connection to a community (a synagogue, for example), there is little motivation and access to further learning and engagement.

Jewish lifecycles drive the 'revolving door' of synagogue membership, namely the *bar/bat mitzvah*. Parents with young children (around age 6 or 7) realize that they need to begin preparations for their child's *bar/bat mitzvah*. Often, this decision is driven by ethnic (historical) and psychological sensibilities. Oftentimes, that history was negative and the psychology is informed by an ethnicity that is regarded as painful. Historically, most synagogues require at least three to four years of religious school training to qualify a child for *bar/bat mitzvah*. Parents will seek out and join a congregation, enroll their child in religious school, have the *bar/bat mitzvah*, and then leave the congregation.[8]

Perhaps if synagogues could explicitly name the value of affiliation at this original moment of connection, they might be able to convert fee-for-service customers into committed community members. Synagogues must be able to express the value of community connection beyond just getting one's son or

---

[6] Ibid, 3.
[7] Ibid, 3.
[8] Steven M. Cohen, "Member and Motives: Who Joins American Jewish Congregations and Why," S3K Report (Fall 2006), 6.

daughter *bar/bat mitzvah*'ed. And, for those who do not consider synagogue affiliation, perhaps hearing an identifiable strand of connecting Jewishness to synagogue will ignite the spark that will direct them to the synagogue community at some later point in their lives. Maybe we could stop this revolving door affiliation if people had reasons to commit to a community.

However, communal commitment is not easy because of a complex and confusing polity structure. Several institutions vie for attention and position. Each has a claim as the focus of Jewish communal identity. The most prominent of these are the synagogue and the Jewish Community Center (JCC). Synagogues function holistically, catering to the nurturing of religious life, study, and community. While an important institution, at best JCC's provide a place for communal gathering. Most have placed primary importance on their roles as health clubs. Nurturing the physical is certainly an important Jewish trait (which most synagogues do not do), but not a holistic approach.

Using ancient Jewish polity language,[9] moving beyond the *kehillah* (synagogue community), the Jewish Federation system functions much the same as *medinoth* (city-state, larger collective of synagogue communities) with local chapters reporting to regional offices, all under the umbrella of the United Jewish Communities (UJC). UJC represents 155 Jewish Federations and 400 independent communities across North America. Also under the umbrella of UJC, are a variety of constituent agencies including the Jewish Council for Public Affairs (JCPA) and their local Jewish Community Relations Council (JCRC) affiliates, Jewish Community Centers, Jewish Council on Aging, Jewish Agency for Israel, American Jewish Joint Distribution Committee, various Hillel (Jewish college ministry) chapters, various Bureau of Jewish Education chapters, and so on.

This complex system of Jewish communal support competes for attention and funding with synagogues. Here, too, is a structure for emulating the *medinoth*. Most American synagogues affiliate with one (sometimes more than one) of the synagogue movements – Union of Reform Judaism (URJ), United Synagogue of Conservative Judaism (USCJ), Union of Orthodox Congregations (OU), and the Jewish Reconstructionist Federation (JRF).[10] Here again, there are local, regional and national offices that support a communal structure.

Contemporary Jews face a confusing morass of communal structure. It is difficult to decide which institutional alignment confers "membership" in the

---

[9]   Daniel J. Elazar, and Stuart A. Cohen, *The Jewish Polity: Jewish Political Organization From Biblical Times to the Present* (Indiana: Indiana University Press, 1985), 13-15.
[10]   There are several other smaller movement affiliates, but these are the four major ones.

community. Can Judaism support two (or more) competing sources for Jewish life and identity? Some say yes, some no. I think a more appropriate question is: where does Jewish identity reside and where can it be nurtured best?

I believe when Jews think of Jewish communal structure, they should think of synagogues as the most important communal institution. As Lawrence Hoffman eloquently states, "I plead for a revival of Jewish culture as religiously important; and I plead for the reinvention of the synagogue as the sole institution with the capacity for reviving it."[11] However, many (if not most) synagogues are stuck in what Hoffman calls "default mode," i.e. doing what they have done for the last fifty years because it is what they have done for the last fifty years! Like the decision of young parents to join a synagogue, this default mode is driven by ethnic sensibilities. However, in order to recover this sense of the religiously important aspects of Jewishness requires us to reclaim Jewish theology. A historical look at Jewish theology helps contextualize this challenge.

Spurred in large measure by a post-World War II desire to understand the nature of evil and the atrocities of Nazi Germany, a new Jewish theology began to emerge. American Judaism particularly did not deal adequately with the problem of evil.[12] The war "helped create among Jewish intellectuals a strong dissatisfaction with established forms of American Jewish thought, and it was responsible for the presence in North America of refugee scholars and theologians who represented new ways of thinking in religion."[13] Additionally, the depth of Christian theological thinking and writing motivated Jewish theological thinking.

This is not to say that there were no Jewish theologians before World War II. Indeed, Jewish theologians had emerged in post-World War I Europe. These included Franz Rosenzweig, Martin Buber, Abraham Joshua Heschel and Joseph Soloveitchik. Most of these thinkers were influenced by the existentialist movement and were contemplating the nature of God in the world from their Jewish perspective. Their audience was not necessarily a Jewish one, at least as far as American Judaism was concerned. In fact, Christian theologians like Reinhold Niebuhr and Paul Tillich were responsible for bringing these Jewish theologians to the attention of an American Jewish audience. Indeed, Will Herberg, one of the initiators of the Jewish intellectual revolution of the 1940s and '50s, became so frustrated by his perception of a lack of serious Jewish theological thought that he

---

[11] Rabbi Lawrence Hoffman, *ReThinking Synagogues: A New Vocabulary for Congregational Life* (Woodstock, Vermont: Jewish Lights, 2006), 9.
[12] Robert G. Goldy, *Emergence of Jewish Theology in America* (Indiana: Indiana University Press, 1990), 3.
[13] Ibid, 2-3.

considered conversion to Christianity. His mentor, Reinhold Niebuhr, encouraged him not to convert and instead direct his theological musings towards Judaism.

Through much of the post-World War II period, particularly the 1940s and '50s, rabbinic seminaries actually had an aversion to theology. Eugene Borowitz writes, "American rabbis have opposed theology because it smacked of pie in the sky and was viewed with traditional skepticism toward preoccupation with hidden things when there was so much to be done with what had already been revealed."[14] Additionally, Borowitz and others feared that theology would emerge as dogmatic and inflexible, and Judaism is allegedly an undogmatic religion.[15] If Jews began eliciting new Jewish theology the "next step would be to seek conformity to it."[16] After a visit to Hebrew Union College (the Reform rabbinical seminary) in 1947, Herberg wrote, "They take theology seriously at H.U.C., but unfortunately their theology is not very serious."[17]

Borowitz also points out that in response to modernism (and post modernism), "Jews have responded more in a social than an intellectual fashion."[18] He remarks that the Jewish movements (akin to denominations in Christianity) respond to issues more ideologically than creating fully developed philosophies of Judaism. "When such issues arise in their (contemporary Jewish intellectuals) work, they do not concentrate their intellectual energies on them and seek to give a systematic – that is, a detailed and coherent – account of what they believe and why."[19] Simply stated, Judaism has no method of creating systematic theological or philosophical positions and no history of attempting to create this. While Borowitz leads me to believe modern Judaism has no capacity for systematic theology, he does identify "systematized positions." These are (with corresponding primary adherents): Neo-Kantianism (Hermann Cohen), Religious Consciousness (Leo Baeck), Nationalism, The Zionist Interpretation of Judaism, Naturalism (Mordecai Kaplan), The Pioneer Existentialist (Franz Rosenzweig), Religious Existentialism (Martin Buber), and Neo-Traditionalism (Abraham Heschel). Borowitz does an excellent job of identifying systematic philosophical positions within Judaism. However, these are uniquely his own and not necessarily shared (nor understood) by a diverse Jewish audience.

---

[14] Eugene Borowitz, "Reform Judaism's Fresh Awareness of Religious Problems: Theological Conference-Cincinnati 1950," Commentary (June 1950), 571.
[15] Robert G. Goldy, Emergence of Jewish Theology in America (Indiana: Indiana University Press, 1990), 13.
[16] Ibid, 13.
[17] Ibid, 8.
[18] Eugene Borowitz, Choices in Modern Jewish Thought (New Jersey: Behrman House, 1995), 17.
[19] Ibid, 18.

In a recent email correspondence with Borowitz, he wrote:

"It also occurred to me that it might be helpful to say a word about the difference between Judaism and Christianity with regard to theology. Christianity is essentially creedal. What you believe is critical to being saved. So, Christians developed abstract thinking about belief - theology. Jewish piety is essentially concerned with how we live, deeds. Thus, our strong literature is Oral Torah, based on what we understand God told us. We do 'theology' only when we find ourselves involved in a culture where philosophy/theology is part of the social order: Alexandria, Spain and Germany/Europe, but not Poland. American Jews have some people, like me, who do theology, but most Jews prefer to shy away from abstract discussions of belief."[20]

Borowitz's characterization concerns Christian theology as a system, whereas my interest is more practical. While I agree that, in theory, Christianity is belief-based and communal secondarily, my experience is that creed is less apparent for many Christians in the works of churches than, say, in worship and lifecycle rituals. It is not my intention to compare and contrast Jewish theology to other religions. Theology for Jews is latent, implicit, unarticulated, and found in practices and ways of life, and what I call implicit knowledge. So, the challenge becomes how to make this theological resource explicit. Even the term "theology" is a barrier to Jews. A better term is "Jewishness", which encompasses identity, culture, history, practice, observance, devotion, ethical perspective, and probably most importantly, a sense of responsibility to the world (*tikkun olam*, to heal or repair the world). By the term "Jewishness", I mean one's Jewish identity (a deep sense) and ways that this is theologically lived in one's life. And, I admit this is an assumption. All of the aforementioned components together comprise Jewishness. In traditions like Christianity and Islam, lived or practiced theology captures this sense. Those terms have little meaning in Judaism. From their study on Jewish spirituality, Cohen and Hoffman remark, "To the extent that we lack a native Jewish language to describe spirituality, we are hampered by having to discuss it in language borrowed from Christianity... Although today it is commonplace to discuss Jewish theology, a generation ago, it was not. If surveyed on whether they had a theology (or what that theology was), most Jews would probably have answered negatively. Though they probably had views about God, they hesitated

---

[20]   Eugene Borowitz, email interview, 22 November 2005.

to use conventional [Christian] language to express them, and, having no other language, could not express them at all."[21]

I want to recover some kind of language for talking about Jewish spirituality in relation to the synagogue. I want to create a method of surfacing the Jewishness (theology) of synagogue affiliation. This implicit value can then be made explicit to those considering affiliation at some point in their lives. What does it mean to be a synagogue member? How does it contribute to one's sense of being a Jew in this culture? Once we are able to get some answers to these questions, we will be able to claim a deeper sense of identity based on synagogue membership.

---

[21] Steven M. Cohen and Lawrence Hoffman, "How Spiritual Are America's Jews? Narrowing the Spirituality Gap Between Jews and Other Americans," S3K Report (March 2009), 4, 14.

NORMS AND VALUES –
DRIVE AND MOTIVATION

There is a shifting in the institutionalization of Judaism. This is hardly the first shift in institutional Judaism. The first, and perhaps most relevant shift, came after the second Temple destruction in 70 A.C.E. At that time, the Diaspora found itself without religious leadership. The rabbis 'transferred' institutional authority from the Temple to the home, and authority from the priesthood to adult householders. In this way, religious practice moved from passive to active – whereas practice was formerly 'performed' by the priesthood, it became a lived experience. The rabbis transferred the power of the *Beit Hamikdash*, house of sanctuary or holiness, to the home – the *Mikdash Me'at,* or little temple. Adult Jews became the new priests. Judaism not only decentralized but also de-institutionalized. Over some years following, synagogues and the rabbinate gained in importance. By the 4th Century A.C.E., the shift back to a form of centralized authority and practice was completely in parallel to the Christianized empire forming centers in grand and majestic churches. In this 300-some year interim, Judaism was celebrated largely as a home-based religion largely for an elite set of rabbis, much the way wealthy Greco-Romans celebrated symposia meals.

According to rabbinic period scholar Jacob Neusner, implicit in this newest shift was a renewed commitment to Jewish religion which took some 300 years (4th century A.C.E. to 1st century C.E.), finalizing in the lifetime of Hillel. By "religion", I am referring primarily to worship and spirituality. Spirituality has become a buzzword and without context, at least for Jews. However, spiritual connection is paramount to the success of modern Judaism and synagogues. In Hoffman's book, he identifies the need for Jews to make spiritual connections within Judaism. He recounts how many young Jews have flocked to eastern religions such as Buddhism and various New Age practices in an attempt to find some kind of spiritual journey or path. While contemporary Christianity has and is attempting to reconcile these disciplines within a context of traditional

Christianity, until recently Judaism has not[22]. Hoffman details the experiences of two converts from Judaism to Christianity. Both were prompted by an inability to "feel the presence of a caring God."[23] While Jews have ethnically done "what comes naturally," many report there is no transcendent purpose with these acts and, therefore, emptiness and vapidity. [24]

Synagogue 2000 (predecessor to Synagogue 3000) showed that ethnicity and religiosity without theology are doomed to failure. It showed that in the long run, ethnicity and religiosity will lose their appeal, particularly for young Jews. Positioned in the context of theology, those cultural and ethnic facets gained the transcendent meaning that modern Jews identify as so important. When positioned within a theological framework, with clear mission and vision postures, transformation became possible. This is new theology for Jews and must be distinguished from the potentially dogmatic and inflexible theology that concerns Borowitz.

Yet, even Synagogue 2000 did not create a language to describe spirituality and connectedness. In its new incarnation, Synagogue 3000, it may do so as a reflection of its previous work. Hoffman calls the method by which the data of Synagogue 2000 might translate into new theological language "pincer thinking." Pincer thinking is defined as "combining Jewish theological categories with the best thought from our own time."[25] This method will reconcile the richness of Jewish text and *midrashic* interpretation with the best of contemporary creativity, and allow us to create a new theological language. The pincer thinking he describes is a way of doing culture; combining traditional Jewish textual sources with contemporary philosophy. And, this new language is not unique to Judaism. This will become a new way of speaking theologically about congregations in their entirety in modern American culture.

Systematic theology separated from practicality often comes out looking ethereal and impracticable. Judaism needs a language from shared experience to communicate meaning and transcendence. Jews have surrendered their ability to talk about relationship with the Divine and words like spirituality, mystical, and transcendence are foreign. Concepts like ministry, vocation, mission, grace, and witness are consigned to Christianity as church-speak. While Judaism certainly has precedent for these concepts, it has no corresponding language or terminology

---

[22] The Institute for Jewish Spirituality was created in 1999, as an example.
[23] Rabbi Lawrence Hoffman, *ReThinking Synagogues: A New Vocabulary for Congregational Life* (Woodstock, Vermont: Jewish Lights, 2006), 57.
[24] Ibid, 5.
[25] Ibid, 8.

with which to speak of them. Consequently, they are replaced by terms from the secular and business world – mission statements, job description, and social justice projects. As Maimonides wrote, humans lack the language to speak of God, and "All these expressions are adapted to the mental capacity of the majority of mankind who have a clear perception of physical bodies only. The Torah speaks in the language of men. All these phrases are metaphorical."[26] Jews have surrendered permission to try. Using secular, business language is at best dysfunctional and, at worst, likens synagogues to a corporate entity.

While population studies diagnose a slow but positive decline in American Jews, synagogues and other Jewish institutions struggle with welcoming new adherents. At the 2005 biennial gathering, Rabbi Eric Yoffie of the Union for Reform Judaism encouraged synagogue leaders to reach out to would-be converts. This comes some twenty-seven years after the Reform movement expressed openness to interfaith couples and families. I think this delay is, in part, due to discomfort with God language. Many potential converts are and have been willing and able to "testify" and "bear witness" to their connection to Judaism. However, Judaism has been unable to hear that testimony, at least in clear God-language. While I applaud Rabbi Yoffie's statement, Judaism still needs that language to communicate the richness and passion of modern American Judaism.

We know that young American Jews are more interested in spirituality. The first study of American Jewish spirituality was completed in 2009, comparing Jewish and non-Jewish spirituality. A Synagogue 3000 (S3K) Report, it is entitled "How Spiritual Are America's Jews?: Narrowing the Spirituality Gap Between Jews and Other Americans." While Jews scored lower than non-Jews in all measurable ways, the trend toward spiritual interest and expression seems evident. Using young Jews as an example, "On the key index of Spiritual Inclination, mean scores rise from 14 among the oldest group, to 22 for the middle-aged, to 27 for those under 35. But, we also observe increases in Spiritual Mentoring, Belief in God, Importance of Religion, and Number of Spiritual Experiences. All five indices register higher scores among the young than the middle-aged, and higher among the middle-aged than the elderly."[27] Interestingly, "younger Jews report lower levels of Jewish association (marriage, friends, neighbors), Jewish affiliation

---

[26] *Mishneh Torah*, Knowledge, Basic Principles, 1:9.
[27] Steven M. Cohen and Lawrence Hoffman, "How Spiritual Are America's Jews? Narrowing the Spirituality Gap Between Jews and Other Americans," <u>S3K Report</u> (March 2009), 10.

(organizations, synagogues, federations, etc.), and Jewish ritual practice (e.g., observance of holidays)."[28]

The report also poses the question of language; are Jews less spiritual or just less able to express their spirituality? "... many Jews are uncomfortable with spirituality. But, is it spirituality or the language of spirituality that they suspect? That issue has come home to us in other areas where the accepted language of discussion sounds Christian: theology, for example."[29]

As long as Jews are uncomfortable with spiritual language, at least that which is perceived as Christian language, Jews will not have a shared vocabulary to discuss sense of meaning and other spiritual questions. Jewishness needs a language. I claim that Jews do have a language of meaning, just not one that is globally shared by all Jews. Those connected to the Jewish community have found ways to make meaning out of their connections, and I seek to find this tacit knowledge and language. Obviously, intermarriage is a critical question in this regard and one that I will address in the conclusion.

---

[28] Ibid, 10.
[29] Ibid, 4.

THE PROJECT

Transformative Actions and Related Strategies

As a way to explore Jewishness and synagogue connection, I undertook a qualitative research project as defined by John Swinton and Harriet Mowat in their book *Practical Theology and Qualitative Research*. Swinton and Mowat explain that qualitative research is "slippery and difficult to contain within a single definition."[30] However, they do 'define' it thusly: "Qualitative research involves the utilization of a variety of methods and approaches which enable the researcher to explore the social world in an attempt to access and understand the unique ways that individuals and communities inhabit it."[31] While admittedly this definition is vague, its vagueness actually compliments the method of my project. Distinguishing qualitative research from other forms of research is, for me, primarily distinguished in the idea that "the world is not simply 'out there' waiting to be discovered"[32], but occurs in the ways in which we choose to view it.

I interviewed a group of eight Jews from a sample of congregations representing the Reform, Conservative and Reconstructionist movements. While including those from the Orthodox tradition might have given a more complete Jewish picture, it might have also skewed the results. More than any other group (and I am generalizing), Orthodox Judaism is comfortable with ethnic attachment. Additionally, the practicing Orthodox are the least likely to "choose" Judaism and synagogue affiliation. Additionally, Orthodox Jews only comprise 12 percent of the total Jewish.[33]

The interviewees represented three distinct categories: synagogue members who are regular worshipers (more than twice a month), those who are regularly

---

[30] John Swinton and Harriet Mowat, *Practical Theology and Qualitative Research* (London: SCM Press, 2007), 29.
[31] Ibid, 29.
[32] Ibid, 29.
[33] Jonathan Ament, "American Jewish Religious Denominations," Rep. United Jewish Communities, n.d, accessed 10 March 2014,
http://www.jewishdatabank.org/Archive/NJPS2000_American_Jewish_Religious_Denominations.pdf.

involved with synagogue life but not necessarily regular worship attendees, and those with irregular involvement.

I looked for patterns. My belief was that Jews who belong to synagogues make tacit theological decisions that inform their Jewishness. These decisions about their membership and participation, including congregational affiliation (or lack thereof), are based on a myriad of unknown cognitive factors. These unknown factors include family history, experience, environment, and socio-economic factors. While social scientists speculate about where and how these factors inform one's religiosity and affiliation, it is speculation. We need to bring these to consciousness in order to move beyond speculation. Moreover, by clarifying these decisions, I believe there lay some practical 'gold' for synagogue communities, enabling them to clearly articulate the value of synagogue affiliation.

The interviewees came from the Midwest area.

	Reform	Conservative	Reconstructionist	Just Jewish
Regular Worshiper	2	1		
Regularly Involved	1	1	1	
Irregular	1			1

The interviews aimed to uncover these possible themes:

1. For those who still affiliate, is this a conscious decision? How much does ethnic sensibility play into their decision? What are the tacit decisions they make that inform their affiliation? Is there a correlation between their decisions to affiliate and the amount of their participation?
2. For those who nominally affiliate, what are the explicit and tacit decisions that inform them?

The Method

Cognitive Task Analysis:

The challenge is to make the tacit knowledge Jews have about their congregational membership decisions explicit. Humans make the tacit become explicit through a process. Truth be told, there are many processes, but so far we are not able to investigate this level of brain awareness beyond one level. Scientists have just begun pursuing this task, making the unconscious purposeful. There are now several terms to denote the process of making the tacit explicit. The founders of its study, including Gary Klein, Robert R. Hoffman, and developmental psychologist Beth Crandall, named it naturalistic decision making (NDM), studying how people actually make decisions and perform cognitively complex functions in demanding situations. These include situations marked by time pressure, uncertainty, vague goals, high stakes, team and organizational constraints, changing conditions, and varying amounts of experience.[34] Klein and Crandall further refined their definition and created the moniker, Cognitive Task Analysis (CTA). CTA has become a catch-all term for the consultative use (as opposed to the theoretical study of) complex decision making. CTA is "a family of methods used for studying and describing reasoning and knowledge."[35] To offer another definition, "Cognitive Task Analysis is a family of methods for understanding the cognitive components of a task."[36]

When humans are performing complex tasks (as opposed to simple tasks such as tying one's shoes, opening a door, etc.), cognitive refers to how people "find out how they think and what they know, how they organize and structure information, and what they seek to understand better."[37] They define a task as "not always the literal action sequences – the steps – that matter as much as the fact that practitioners are trying to get things done; they are not simply performing sets of procedures."[38] Finally, they define analysis as the act of analyzing something "to break it into parts in order to understand both the component parts and their relationship in making up the whole."[39] In summation, "cognitive task analysis

---

[34] Gary Klein, Sources of Power: How People Make Decisions (Massachusetts: The MIT Press, 1998), 4.

[35] Beth Crandall, Gary Klein, Robert R. Hoffman, Working Minds: A Practitioners Guide to Cognitive Task Analysis (Massachusetts: The MIT Press, 2006), 3.

[36] Klein Associates, Getting the Story Behind the Story: Putting Cognitive Task Analysis to Work , 6.

[37] Crandall, Klein, Hoffman, 3.

[38] Ibid, 3.

[39] Crandall, Klein, Hoffman, 3.

methods provide procedures for systematic, scientific experimentation to support description and understanding."[40]

In his book *Blink: The Power of Thinking Without Thinking,* author Malcolm Gladwell creates the term "thin-slicing", which he defines as "the ability of our unconscious to find patterns in situations and behavior based on very narrow slices of experience."[41] Gladwell likens thin-slicing to mind reading as a practical skill that everyone possesses. Instead of mind reading reserved for those with extra sensory perception or some other extra human, other worldly skill, mind reading is really the ability to use one's experience and innate knowledge to make predictions about people's actions and behavior. I hoped to uncover patterns of thin-slicing in these interviews. I will report the 'thin-slicing' of the interviewees. I posit that these thin slices of experience are central to getting in touch with our own tacit knowledge. I believe that by using CTA, it is possible to solicit definable evidence of how and why people's decisions inform their theological worldview, i.e. their relationship to God and their synagogue community.

I am especially interested in the question of why Jews are involved in synagogues and why they bother to join and remain enjoined to them. Why do people join and remain enjoined to synagogues? We know Jewish worship attendance is minimal when compared to church worship (less than 10%)[42]. Why, then, are they involved in synagogues? I contend that there are deep theological reasons why Jews 'belong' to synagogues, and that these reasons are tacit and unconscious. Using the approach of CTA and thin-slicing, I expected to uncover the tacit knowledge that will help get at this information in a way that other methods have not.

Formulating questions ahead of time is somewhat counter to CTA. Interview questions using CTA feed from each previous question. The idea is to ask questions that cause the interview subject to think deeply, and then ask probing questions related to their answers. However, I used some common questions as starting points and benchmarks:

- Name a positive experience you've had at your congregation.
- Think back to the moment when you decided to make this congregation your "spiritual home." What were some of the attributes that attracted you to the congregation?

---

[40] Ibid, 3.
[41] Malcolm Gladwell, Blink: The Power of Thinking Without Thinking (New York: Little, Brown & Co, 2005), 23.
[42] George Conger, "Poll: US Jews uninterested in shul," The Jerusalem Post, 20 April 2006, Accessed 1 March 2009, http://www.jpost.com/Jewish-World/Jewish-News/Poll-US-Jews-uninterested-in-shul

- Tell me about an experience in this congregation when you felt most alive, most fulfilled, or most enthused.
- Can you recall an experience when you felt a deep sense of belonging in the congregation?
  - Was it a sense of being part of something bigger than yourself?
  - Something led by God (higher power, spiritual sense, etc.)?
- What comes to mind when you hear the word "spirituality"?
  - What are the things that you would consider "spiritual"?
    - (are they related by ethnic identity or some kind of sympathetic, obligatory sense they have to heritage)
- Was there a spiritual background to your childhood?

The nature of CTA makes these questions starting points only. For instance, if the respondent cannot name a positive experience, the direction of the interview may go to negative experiences and discovery of the respondent's sense of ethnic responsibility rather than connectedness to community. Conversely, a respondent may be able to identify ethnic and cultural childhood memories that he or she considers deeply spiritual. The conversation would then explore the nature of spirituality for this person and if these experiences truly have transcendent meaning. I was careful not to use these set questions to influence or sway the direction of the conversations. They were merely thematic, topical elements allowing for comparison of one interview to another, and a way to allow me to keep the conversation going.

Cues[43] are critical to CTA. I looked for the following during the interviews:

a. What were the subjects' emotional responses? Were they congruent with their verbal responses? CTA/CDM (Cognitive Decision Making) calls these ambiguous cues, strategies, anomalies/violated expectations.

b. What were the subjects' non-verbal responses (body positioning, eye movement, hand-wringing, tearfulness, etc.)?

c. Were the subjects answering a technical question with deeply emotional or psychoanalytical (adaptive) answers?

d. Were the answers disproportional to the question? Similar to above, but an example might be if the subject goes off on an unrelated, tangential issue rather than sticking to the subject of the question.

---

[43] CTA cues include signals such as body movements, eye connection (or lack of), speech patterns, etc. It would also include refusal, overt or covert, to directly address questions.

e. Critical decision points – did subjects make decisions at some point in their lives that might influence their current beliefs? These decision points could move the interviews into a more pure CDM method, whereby focusing on the decision will inform the conversation and outcomes.

f. Did the person make a decision about something (maybe at a critical decision point) and then attach meaning to it? For example, they decided that their religious education was adequate and therefore considered themselves Jewish experts, requiring no further explication or exploration of Judaism.

Identifying participants:

In order to identify interviewees, I sent an email to 205 recipients. This list was a random sampling of people in the Midwest. Of the 205 who received the survey, 64 responded (details included in Appendix I). The survey provided a baseline of information, as well as clearly defined who fell into the affiliated/connected/active criteria posed above. From the 64, I chose the 8 interviewees.

I made recordings of each interview (with permission). While CTA is nebulous and hard to describe, its progression is quite organic and fascinating to experience.

A contextual tool:

Just before the interview, I administered another tool: the Implicit Association Test (IAT), also borrowed from Gladwell's book *Blink*. As Gladwell explains, the IAT evaluates an individual's tacit biases (https://implicit.harvard.edu/implicit/demo). IAT is a part of Harvard University's "Project Implicit". The purpose of Project Implicit is described on their website:

> *"Project Implicit represents a collaborative research effort between researchers at Harvard University, the University of Virginia, and University of Washington. While the particular purposes of each study vary considerably, most studies available at Project Implicit examine thoughts and feelings that exist either outside of conscious awareness or outside of conscious control. The primary goals of Project Implicit are to provide a*

safe, secure, and well-designed virtual environment to investigate psychological issues and, at the same time, provide visitors and participants with an experience that is both educational and engaging."[44]

The IAT's are a series of tests that measure an individual's bias towards or from distinct societal groups. For instance, there are tests to measure one's reactions to political candidates, people with disabilities, ethnic groups, racial groups, religious groups, heavy/thin people, etc. There is a test that measures bias towards or from certain religions: "Religion ('Religions' IAT). This IAT requires some familiarity with religious terms from various world religions (https://implicit.harvard.edu/implicit/Study?tid=-1). This IAT requires the ability to recognize religious symbols from various world religions."[45] IAT's are taken online without a moderator (other than someone to aid the individual in getting started). They use a series of pictures, symbols and representations, and time the participant's reaction (negative or positive) to them. I took this religion test and discovered I have a bias towards Jewish symbols and representations. This is not surprising, except my bias towards Judaism includes a bias away from other religions.

I asked the CTA interviewees to complete the test before the interview. These provided both a benchmark for the interviewee answers, and as a way to measure how much Jewish communal membership is a reaction away from other religious groups rather than towards Judaism.

---

[44] Project Implicit: Background Information,
https://implicit.harvard.edu/implicit/backgroundinformation.html.
[45] Project Implicit: Demonstration Tests, https://implicit.harvard.edu/implicit/demo/selectatest.html.

THE INTERVIEWS

As mentioned in the introduction, I sent a survey to a random sampling of people in the Midwest. Of the 205 who received the survey, 64 responded.[46] From the 64, I chose the eight interviewees to match my sample population category. Interviewees were selected using two main criteria; movement affiliation and regularity of attendance.

I tried to divide the eight equitably by national movement affiliation. As reported by the American Jewish Religious Denominations report of the 2005 National Jewish Population Survey, 33% of Jews affiliate Reform, 26% Conservative, 0.02% Reconstructionist, and 25% just Jewish. Therefore, of the eight interviewees, four were Reform, two Conservative, one Reconstructionist, and one just Jewish.

The interviewees matched the following attributes:[47]

	Male	Female	Age 26-39	Age 40-65	Reform	Conservative	Reconstructionist	Just Jewish	Regular in worship	Regular involvement	Irregular
Arnie	X			X	X				X		
Esther		X		X	X					X	
Vince	X			X	X				X		
Aviva		X			X					X	
Michelle		X		X			X			X	
Sheila		X	X					X			X
Marcie		X		X	X						X
Sam	X		X		X				X		

---

[46] See Appendix 1.
[47] Note: this table shows the primary attribute for interviewees. For example, they might have identified themselves as a regular worshiper and regularly involved.

22

I asked to meet each person at their place of business or home. This was, in part, to give a sense of comfort (somewhere familiar) and for quiet. Recording the conversations was paramount, as CTA does not lend itself to taking a lot of notes. It was important for me to stay focused on the responses, in order to formulate questions that would go deeper into the interviewee's experience, soliciting their tacit knowledge.

Before the interview began, I asked each participant to take the Religion IAT (https://implicit.harvard.edu/implicit/Study?tid=-1). My hope was that the IAT would provide both a benchmark for the interviewee answers, and as a way to measure how much Jewish communal membership is a reaction away from other religious groups rather than towards Judaism. The IAT took about ten minutes.

The interview write-ups that follow are certainly not verbatim, and I took quite a bit of editing license. Informal speech (which is what I hoped to engender from the interview subjects) is messy, full of um's and uh's, pauses, stammering, etc. that does not read well. To that end, I condensed and combined the verbiage of each answer. However, my goal was only to make the answers more readable and not change the substance of the answers. In some cases, I left words like "cuz" instead of "because", "yeah" instead of "yes", etc. because they seemed truer to the spirit of the conversation. In some cases, I added inferred words or phrases in parentheses. In many cases, I eliminated phrases like "you know," "I mean," etc.

Most of the time, the write-ups are structured in narrative fashion broken by paragraphs. For readability sake, in some spots I switched to script layout using "Me:" and "[Interviewee's name]." This mostly occurs when there is a direct back and forth exchange of dialogue that stands on its own.

It should be noted that eight interviews is hardly a broad, scientific sampling. However, between preparations, doing the interview, reviewing the transcription of each interview and writing them up, each took an average of eight to ten hours. Doing more than eight is simply beyond the scope of this project. Nevertheless, I was looking for patterns, insights, cues and language that might predict tangible, perceptible and substantive tools that synagogues might use to attract members.

It also should be noted that I did not use the interviewee's real names. While several expressed no issues with identity, several were very clear that my using their real name was an issue and they would be uncomfortable. Again, my goal was to elicit honest, genuine responses, and making the interviewees as comfortable as possible was paramount.

Arnie

Arnie is one interviewee who does not have deep generational ties to the Jewish community in which he currently lives. He came to the city less than seven years ago when his wife took a job in one of the city's suburbs. He is in the 40 – 65 age range, identifies himself as a Conservative Jew, his wife is Jewish and they have one young child. He attended Hebrew and Sunday school, went to Jewish camp, and was a member of a Jewish youth group.

Arnie described his upbringing as "Classic Reform." In the next sentence, he says he was "always eager to learn more about Judaism and felt that we were perhaps more liberal and I wanted to be more observant than my parents." He followed by talking about searching where he fits in the spectrum of Judaism and came to the determination that he is "not real fond of the boxes" that are Reform, Conservative, Orthodox, etc. He pointed out that his upbringing gave him a good background, but was quick to distinguish it from what he is giving his child. His son attends Jewish day school and they hope he will continue to Jewish high school and beyond. Arnie stated how important it would be for his child to marry someone Jewish. He said, "I could deal with him being gay more than him not marrying someone who's Jewish... as long as his gay partner is Jewish."

Traditions were important in his family of origin – keeping Shabbat, Passover *seder*, having *bar mitzvah*, going to religious school, etc. He shared that his parents were active in the synagogue, especially religious school. He related that what his family gave him was a Jewish mindset and that the way he sees the world is Jewish. "I can't modify that... my eyes see Jewish." When asked if he had a sense that someone gave him permission to see the world this way, Arnie answered, "No, I feel like I've been fighting my whole life to think this way."

I asked Arnie if he could identify the point in his life when he came to feel uncomfortable with the Jewish worldview of his family of origin. With some pressing, he identified a time in his late 20's when he developed "a sense of security with myself and the path that I'm following, where I see that spirituality is definitely a journey, not a straight line, with curves and twists, and going backwards is going forwards... it was just an adult concept for me, that this journey is OK." When asked if this transition included affiliation with a synagogue, he answered that he has always been connected with some kind of synagogue community. The particular community that enabled his 'maturing' Jewish worldview was a Humanistic synagogue he joined in his early – mid 20's.

He attributes this community with allowing him to feel permission to use his brain more and be open to other interpretations of Judaism. He also shared that first and perhaps foremost, the community was a small group. "I seem to do better in small, spiritual groups than a mega whatever." It was also a new movement and it was exciting for him to be part of a pioneering group that was defining its own rules and systems; "what do we want, what do we not want, how are we going to define this?"

He shared there was newness, openness, and a permission to think differently, and "a reassurance that I was valued with my opinion." The rabbi also affirmed this permission. When I asked if the rabbi nurtured this free thinking, he said that nurture was not the right word, it was more "an energy" that permeated the community. The rabbi was young, as were all the community members. "We were all colleagues... and that felt comfortable." There was a permission to "say what you want and we can share ideas... listen and try to figure things out."

When I asked Arnie if he felt a part of something bigger than himself during that time, he said "yeah, I was able to add, change or color something that at that time I don't think you could get if you walked into one of the bigger *shuls*." He reported that their little community was affecting something more than just itself – it was affecting Judaism as a whole. For Arnie, defining themselves as humanistic did not have the same labeling aspect. Indeed, it seemed to be anti-label. The lack of structure added to his comfort.

From this new, nurturing, humanistic community, Arnie moved (for work) to a new city that had a very small Jewish community. "The first Friday night in a new city... okay, what am I going to do? Well, I'll try the synagogue. And, in the parking lot people came up to me and totally blew me away – 'you must be Arnie'... I got twelve phone calls from people I didn't even know... who said 'come and have *Rosh Hashanah* dinner with us', 'have lunch with us', 'do you want to sit with us at *shul*?'... I felt wonderful... I'd made a good decision (to move there)." Arnie related that it was this sense of small community which led him to choose his current congregation. Arnie subsequently married and his wife's job brought them to their current location.

Upon arrival in their new home, Arnie shared that he and his wife did the requisite "synagogue hopping", but only found the sense of smallness at one congregation. When pressed to define smallness, he said it is the sense that "you need to be a participant and not an observer." The sense that it was the "little group where you aren't lost" drove their decision to join his current, Conservative affiliated synagogue.

In conversations with the rabbi before joining, Arnie told him that he did not think he believed in all the tenets of Conservative Judaism. The rabbi told him, "There are other ways of looking at a synagogue." He reminded him that there were many aspects of a congregation beyond dogma and ritual such as "... peer groups, the social and volunteering aspects." Arnie realized that community size, intimacy, and relatedness could trump dogma. Not only did this get him in the door, but he says it has now enabled him to broaden his study and look at new ways of being Jewish; some he has adopted, some not.

Arnie repeatedly described community as essential to his life. He sees community in concentric circles, with the innermost including his son and wife, the next their extended families, then his synagogue community, the city's Jewish community, state, nation, etc. Interestingly, Arnie reported getting "flack from my family" about his increased observance. His sister regularly says, "This is not how we did this, this is not how you were brought up." While they remain close, Arnie thinks that his family is somehow challenged by his decision to be more observant, but he does not feel the need to defend these decisions.

When asked about spirituality and whether he feels that sense at synagogue, he answered that yes, at times spirituality is a part of his life in the congregation. Oftentimes, though, "it's just hanging out with a bunch of Jews." Arnie talked about helping to cook in the synagogue's kitchen and how connected he feels both to his fellow cooks and to the synagogue community. When I pressed him on his definition of spirituality, he admitted that, indeed, these communal experiences are spiritual moments, though he is not always aware of it at the time. He shared that he is learning that spirituality is a sense of belonging to something greater than oneself and a sense of connectedness. In that vein, he realized that even during his period of time in the humanistic community, there were spiritual experiences. Though he quickly said "no" when I asked if he had had any spiritual experiences as a child, when offered in the terms of relatedness or connectedness to something greater, he seemed to agree that his participation in youth group and other synagogue activities gave him a sense of belonging and connectedness. He was also quick to add that, "even there (youth group), you got to explore and write your own service and explore new music, spend late nights talking and being Jewish." Again, Arnie connected the themes of creativity, individuality and empowerment to connectedness and belonging.

Arnie is far from what I would term a Jewish exclusivist. Quite the contrary, he relayed experimenting with other religions, even going to Bible study with Christian friends. Arnie's IAT results bear this out. According to the IAT, he views Judaism and Christianity as equal, with Buddhism and Islam equal and not far below. His experimentation led him back to Judaism, and a Judaism that is more traditional than that of his childhood. Even this eventuality was part of a discovery.

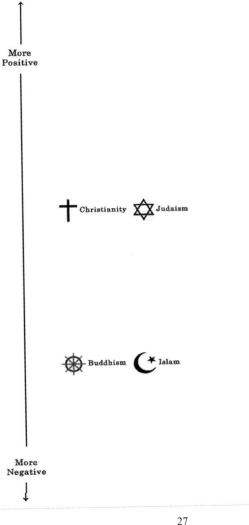

Your Implicit Preference Scale

I did not get a sense that Arnie is led by a strong sense of ethnic identity. He seemed to have little ethnic connection to the "old country"; all but one of his grandparents were born in America, and even his great grandparents were born here. While I would characterize Arnie as fairly Jewishly educated, he did not have a strong sense of 'Yiddishness' often found in American Ashkenazic (of Eastern European origin) Jews. In some respects, his parents' affiliation with Classic Reform eschewed those Yiddish labels and negated the passing of them to Arnie and his sister. While he certainly shares the affinity for "Jewish food" and customs of Yiddish culture, it does not seem accompanied by obligation as much as choice. Arnie seems to have spent time exploring, searching, and learning about Judaism and making choices based thereon.

Arnie's patterns and insights were clear. Connection to the Jewish community is paramount for him. Synagogue size is of major importance to him, namely the synagogue must be small and have a sense of familiarity and intimacy. It is also evident that valuing individuality is important to Arnie.[48] From individuality comes empowerment, at least at the level of free thinking and free expression of thought. Arnie expressed several times that throughout his life, it was important for his ideas to be heard and considered, even if challenged. One might surmise from these characteristics that relationships are very important to Arnie and his prerequisites for a relational community are small size, a community that fosters intimacy, a community that values individuality, and a community that empowers and engenders free thinking.

---

[48]   I think it important to point out here when mentioning concepts like "a sense of connectedness" and "individuality" that I was not inferring ideas for interviewees as much as offering examples. My hope was that they felt license to correct me or challenge the concepts. It is also important to point out that by "tacit knowledge" I am using it to mean knowledge one already has versus discovering new knowledge. This is in line with Klein et al.'s concept of tacit knowledge.

Aviva

Aviva was born in Israel. Her family immigrated to Canada when she was in middle school, and later moved to the Midwest United States where she met, married and has settled with her husband and children. She is in the 40 to 65 age range, is affiliated with a synagogue, and considers herself a Conservative Jew. She is a regular worship attendee and very active in other synagogue affairs.

When I asked Aviva to name a positive synagogue experience, without hesitation she named her daughter's *bat mitzvah*. When I pressed for specifics about what made it positive, she replied, "All of it, from the service to the warmth of the congregation, to the joy of watching her reach that milestone, to how well she engaged in it."

When I asked her to name a time when she felt alive, fulfilled, engaged or connected in the synagogue, she was less decisive about her answer. She gave a vague, general answer of holiday and lifecycle celebrations, especially those where she has taken an active role in the service. She honed in on the word "connected" and replied that, "I get that [sense of connectedness] a lot in synagogue. The connection to the people that are there, the people that had been there before, those that will come thereafter, very connected in that way." She was unable to describe connectedness, so I asked her to put a feeling to it. She said it felt peaceful. When pressed, she described this as a "feeling of being home... It feels like home, you know. My place just, like, where I like to sit on my couch watching TV, that's my spot. I have my spot in the synagogue... when I walk into the building, I feel like I'm walking into something that is part of my life." I asked if she ever had this same feeling at other synagogues or at other places. She replied that she did, especially in Israel and specifically at the Western Wall, "...down to the location in the courtyard that's mine."

I asked Aviva if this sense of connection and belonging was part of something bigger than her. She said yes, "...it's really a connection in the chain. [There's] not any better way of explaining it. Of being part of something that connects me to my parents, grandparents, and great grandparents that I didn't even know (and some that I did), to my children, and hopefully future generations as well. But, in many ways, connection to the people as well, of (in my case) the Jewish faith. It has nothing specifically to do with the faith, but a connection to all before, during, and hopefully, the future."

Working off this chain of ancestry analogy, I asked what might be the links in the chain; what are the things that connect people. It was difficult for her to formulate a clear answer, though she described it as an emotional connection; that even though she did not know some of her ancestors, she still feels an attachment to them. I asked if she thought her parents had this same sense of connection, and she said yes. However, when I asked if they talked about it she said, "a little."

I asked her how she thought she received this sense of connection if her parents did not talk about it. She described it as an innate sense of responsibility, "... it's part of just the way we are. You don't have to have a lot of conversations to have that understanding... the sense of responsibility, and relationship to the Jewish people. It's just part of the makeup. It's one more thing that we're about."

Again, pressing for clarity around this innate sense, I asked to whom and what she was responsible. She replied, "Whatever the need may be that I can fulfill. So, [it] depends... from having someone to dinner that doesn't have a place to go, to financially assisting when we can and others can't. And, things that make life easier for Jews." And again, pressing this innate sense, I asked if she thought she learned this from her parents. "I think that my parents modeled that responsibility, as did my grandparents. So, I was raised with that's how you live your life. Yes, I did learn it." I asked if these were stated expectations or implicit. She answered, "Mostly implicit, but other times made clear. This was what we do."

I asked Aviva if she felt that she was part of something bigger than herself in regards to her community or synagogue. She answered yes, she was part of her extended family and the Jewish community, "that's all bigger than me." I asked if God is included in that. She answered, "oh, absolutely" and said "I believe in God... then that's certainly more than little old me."

I asked her reaction to the word "spirituality". Aviva said, "spirituality is inner faith, personal lifting. It could be personal, or communal, or whatever. But, when you said it at first, I thought of it on an individual basis." I asked what she meant by lifting; from where to where? "Internally, from a feeling of the mundane of what we do, day in and day out, to a higher level of experience, and that may just come out as a personal warmth and fulfillment. Truly, enlightenment may be a level of depth of connectedness to God and people in a way that I don't achieve yet, [laugh]."

I asked if there were things that she does or that happen in her life that she would call spiritual. "Yeah, I think there are moments where I feel spiritual, with

30

that warmth, that better sense of self, a better version of me. Yeah, I think that I have those moments, fleeting as they may be. But, I certainly can think of those moments with the word connectedness, because I spiritually feel connected." I asked Aviva if she thought spirituality was learned or innate. She answered, "I don't know if it's innate or it's developed, but I think that certainly, certain customs are designed to connect to that. And, I think that there's a certain kind of, it's not meditation that occurs, but for lack of a better word, when you *daven*[49] and pray, that gets you in that rhythm. That opens that up, that opportunity. And, the more you do it, suddenly, you're *davening*, and I think someone had taught me how to do that. Or, showed me how it was done, and I either copied it or repeated it in a way that suddenly became my own."

I asked if there were other experiences that elicited this sense, and Aviva described being up at 2 AM with her children when they were babies. I asked if in those moments she had a sense of connectedness beyond the one to one relationship with a child. She replied "absolutely," and followed with "I'm shocked and lifted by it. Outside of religious institutions, I think there's lots of spirituality that occurs at the home. Last night, lighting the candles, we had people around us for Hanukkah; we had a group of Jewish friends and a couple that, I don't know what their religion is, and a mother and two daughters that are Christian. And, at the end, we held hands, and let them say what they usually say, which shocked the mother. The daughter we knew had something to say. And, I think those are great moments of spirituality."

I asked Aviva if she felt her synagogue was her spiritual home. She said "No, I don't think I'd call anyplace the spiritual home." I then asked what attributes attracted her to this congregation. She answered, "… to start with, the people. And, then the type of service… the camaraderie that occurs, and warmth, and the welcoming feeling." She shared that this is not her first synagogue affiliation in the city and that she was even part of the leadership of another synagogue. She shared that she "didn't know the people" (at the other synagogue) and felt their approach did not foster knowing others. Her move to her current synagogue was predicated by its approach of, "welcomed… it's a much more hands-on synagogue."

I asked Aviva if she could name a point in her life where she made a discernible choice about the kind of synagogue she wanted. "I don't think that I can pinpoint a moment that's 'okay, I want this', and 'I want that'. But, as I grew, there were things that I liked and didn't like. And, I was trapped in those things I

---

49   Eastern European Yiddish verb meaning "to pray."

liked and tried to distance myself from those I didn't. So, that's kind of how it evolved. [Then there] was the question of 'where would you want to raise your children'? 'What would you like them to be a part of'? And, my synagogue is part of the imprint I want to have on them... so, when they compare things, that's their basis."

Referring back to Aviva's survey answers, I pointed out that for the question, "Being Jewish adds meaning to my life", she answered "strongly agree." But, for the question "Synagogue membership is essential to my Jewishness", she chose "disagree." I asked if she saw a disconnect between being Jewish and being a member of a synagogue. She shared that one was her Jewishness, the other her affiliation. "The building, the structure isn't essential for my feeling of fulfillment. It certainly helps, and I love my synagogue. And, I've taken roles in that synagogue. So, the disconnect is not an essential element."

At this point in the interview, while I was unsatisfied with Aviva's answers, it was also clear from her nonverbal cues that she was not willing to dig any deeper into the issues. There appeared to be, for her, a tension between her sense of Jewishness and what she subsequently called her "secular Zionist" sensibility. Aviva offered that, for her, Judaism is not a choice. "… it's just part of what is. So, I don't see it as a choice. I don't see it as a non-choice. It's like, why be human."

Switching gears somewhat to practice (with which she seemed more willing and comfortable to talk about), I asked about religiosity, using the lighting of the Sabbath candles as an example (that she offered). She shared that "there is something spiritual about lighting the *Shabbos* candles. I think it does divide the mundane from the non-mundane. And, I remember my socialist-Zionist grandfather making sure that his wife (my grandmother) lights the *Shabbos* candles on Friday nights. Now, he wouldn't get up and be in the room with her and it didn't mean anything to him other than, of course, it always had to be done. So, it's part of the connectedness to the Jewish people; a knowledge that that's happening everywhere around the world at about the same time. To me, that's a connection that occurs every Friday. I like that a lot."

I asked Aviva to be her grandfather for the moment and asked: "What is it about lighting those candles that connects him to the Jewish people?" "I would suspect that that connected him to his life in Romania beforehand. I think he probably connected it to things that he would rather not say. As a socialist-Zionist, to move to the British mandated creation of the state of Israel was to fulfill his Zionistic dreams... I think it just was part of the same reason he couldn't tell me why Jerusalem was non-negotiable. So, I think that there's a connection in the physical action of lighting. I think it was a memory. For him, it's just what you do. As with the sense of obligation/responsibility."

I asked Aviva what makes her Jewish. She replied quickly, "Birth." I said nothing and she added, "And, the way I live my life. I mean, I would suspect that everybody who's ever met me would consider me Jewish." I encouraged Aviva to elaborate.

Aviva: Jews are a "… group of people that have a common heritage, language and purpose in the world."

Me: "And, what's the purpose?"

Aviva: "… to leave the world better than they found it."

Me: "How do you do that?"

Aviva: "By taking care of your own and others; by improving the life of everyone you come in contact with."

Me: "Don't other religions do that?"

Aviva: "They might."

Me: "Is there a uniquely Jewish way that Jews do that?"

Aviva: "I saw a video of the Israeli Air Force flying over Auschwitz. And, you know, they're flying over… then they do the one bearing to the left, and then he lands in Auschwitz. In 60 seconds, he passed 60 years of history. I think there's something unique about that. I think there's something Jewish about that… we do that in ways that reach out beyond just a select group. It's not about converting others to Judaism. … so, when you go to Ethiopia and you meet with people who don't look anything like you, I think there's something very Jewish about that. I think there's something very Jewish about Menachem Begin saying (his first act as prime minister) that the Vietnamese boat people have a place to come ashore. I think that's very Jewish, even though it had nothing to do with Jews."

While Aviva had some patterns and insights that matched other interviewees, the conversation was frustrating for me because of her seeming inability to dig into the roots of her answers. She repeatedly gave me what seemed pat answers, and gave no indication that she was taking time to think about her responses. I had to remind myself that while she is American now, she grew up in Israel and her extended family is Israeli. My experience is that Israelis have a

33

nationalism akin to American nationalism, but one that conflates with their Jewish identity. This certainly appeared to be the case with Aviva, and I think her IAT score (Figure below) bears this out. While she spoke highly of other religions, Judaism scored markedly higher than other religions. While she did her best to answer my questions, oftentimes I felt she was answering perfunctorily and telling me what she thought I wanted to hear.

Your Implicit Preference Scale

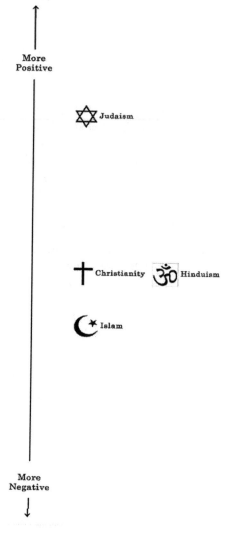

I sensed a tension between her Israeli Judaism and her American Judaism. It is interesting to note that she concluded our conversation by offering: "I think these are questions that people should be asking themselves. I mean, as a community, we should be asking ourselves these questions... You know, the world throws at us change, and yet we remain the same in some ways. I think we need to be asking ourselves [about] that, and we don't engage enough in that conversation." Even in this statement there seems a paradox between changing and staying the same.

More than some interviewees, Aviva was very comfortable talking about spirituality. While I sometimes sensed a conflation of spirituality and practice, she would ultimately explain that practice gave her access to connectedness. I consider this her American Judaism. Her Israeli Judaism is then characterized by that inability to dig deeper into what she considers an innate (and ultimately inexplicable and possibly inherited) sense of responsibility to the Jewish people. While at first I likened this to Hoffman's characterization of ethnicity (and there is some of that sense present), I now think it is more of Aviva's Israeli nationalism that, if challenged, might force her to challenge her very sense of self. That is beyond the scope of this study.

With this said, Aviva did offer some insights. For her, synagogue needs to offer a sense of comfort. While she did not name it, relationships seem a driving force for her connection to a congregation. She illustrated this with her departure from one synagogue to join another. The first offered her no outlet for forming new and lasting relationships. The second congregation was founded on principles of relationship building.

Esther

Esther is affiliated with a Reform synagogue and considers herself a Reform Jew. She is in the 40-65 age range and has lived in her current location for over 20 years. Esther attends worship sporadically and while she has been an active congregational leader, is not currently. After an extended period of service and regular activity at the synagogue, Esther and her husband took a hiatus from synagogue membership. Just before taking the survey for this project, they began conversations about recommitting to membership again. While not a lifelong resident, she and her husband raised both of their children in town and consider themselves natives.

When I asked Esther to identify a positive synagogue experience, her answer was: "I love the music." When I asked for something more specific, her answer was: "If anything makes me feel spiritual at synagogue... it's the music." Again, I asked for specifics, and Esther could not name a person or piece of music that was readily identifiable, but then she shared: "back when I was a kid, we [the synagogue of her childhood] had a choir and the soloist who was, very interestingly, a paid soloist and not Jewish; she had an operatic voice and was astounding. She was amazing. So, I always remembered as a kid really being impressed and liking that."

I asked if there was anything else that might give her the same feeling as music in her current synagogue. She shared that she and her family used to attend a yearly Rosh Hashanah retreat at a local Jewish camp. When I asked what about that experience sticks with her, she replied "the setting." I asked, "what about the setting?" She replied, "Oh, it was beautiful, it was outdoors and to be quite honest, you got to move around a lot too which made the day easier." I asked if aesthetics were important to Esther and she quickly replied "yes." Then she followed with, "But, also, and this is hard for me, I'm a very traditional person and that's why I want to be appropriate and respectful when I'm talking about those services. My daughter went to services recently in Portland, Oregon. This was High Holy Days services. There was, like, modern dance interpretation and things like that, and it drove her crazy. And, I would not like that either. I like the liturgy, and I like the order of things, and I like the service to be what in my mind is a Jewish service." I replied, "Which is? Can you articulate that?" She said, "I'm not sure I can, but certainly it's got to contain the prayers, you know the traditional prayers that accompany the service. And, I think just a certain respectfulness about the proceedings. You know, it doesn't bother me to have a guitar and sing along at the service or something like that. Some people don't really like them when they feel campy. I guess it doesn't bother me too much as long as it's a fairly traditional service."

I asked what was un-traditional about interpretive dance. "I don't know. It's just not something that... I'm probably using the word traditional as a substitute for what I'm accustomed to, and I'm not accustomed to seeing interpretive dance as part of a worship service." I asked, "Would you go so far as to say that that kind of expression is un-Jewish?" She replied, "No, I wouldn't say it's un-Jewish. I wouldn't. I don't want to say it's disrespectful, but it's not... It's not... Again, probably just not what I would expect to see in a Jewish service." I responded, "So, uncomfortable? It's not comfortable for you?" Esther said, "Right."

Following on the theme of comfort, I asked Esther if she felt comfortable at her current synagogue. She replied, "Mostly yes" and then quickly followed with, "I wasn't hugely thrilled with the rabbi, although he was okay. I was very put off by the politics and the rabbi turning. That's one of the reasons that [my husband] and I decided to take a break. I was on the board for a number of years there and, interestingly, even at the board level, a lot of the politics were sorta sub-radar. Rabbi [previous] left fairly shortly after I left the board, and I was not aware of any of the stuff going on regarding him, but obviously there had been among the upper echelons of the board. You know, [on] any board there's going to be politics and all that, but somehow you wish you could be above that for certain things. But, it doesn't work that way. As a matter of fact, this was maybe one of the most political and ineffective boards I've ever served on." Since I wanted to stay on the theme of comfort and knowing we would get to her leadership experience, I asked to suspend the board experience conversation to later in the interview.

I asked Esther about the Judaism of her childhood and if her current congregation is similar to the one of her childhood. She said it was and that her experience of Judaism as an adult is similar to that of her parents. "I grew up in a Reform household, did not regularly attend services, went [to synagogue] on the high holidays and, of course, *bat mitzvah* and other special events. We did light the *Shabbat* candles every Friday night, did not go out Friday nights even through high school. No going out on dates, whatever on Friday nights. [I] went to Hebrew school, got *bat mitzvahed*, Sunday schooled, the whole nine yards. So, yeah, that's what I'm used to." It is interesting to note here that to the survey question "In terms of my religious upbringing, I was raised..." Esther's answer was "Reform, so raised Jew 'ish'."

I followed with a question about her parents' upbringing and asked if it was similar to hers. She answered no, that her mother was a Holocaust survivor and orphaned at 12. She was raised "observant" until orphaned and then in a Conservative synagogue. Esther shared that when her parents married, they decided to be a Reform household.

I asked Esther if there was an experience in synagogue when she felt alive or fulfilled. With some hesitation she shared, "That's the problem for me... another one of the reasons that we are disaffiliated right now. That it's [synagogue] worthy of your time, energy and dollars. It's hard for me to think of any time that I've really, really, felt spiritually moved in a synagogue. And, I'm very conflicted about that because I understand the need in Judaism, or any organized religion, for communal prayer, for communal gathering. But, it does nothing for me, and it's a problem for me. And, the God I believe in is not a deterministic God, and that makes prayer very difficult... It's, you know, what is prayer if the God on the other side does not hear or respond, at least on a personal level. So, finding spiritual uplift inside the synagogue is something that has eluded me." Another item of note: I had not mentioned the words "spirituality" or "God" yet.

I asked Esther if she ever felt alive or fulfilled at the *Rosh Hashanah* Jewish camp experience. She replied, "Yeah, I liked that a lot, but probably that was more of a social thing. Certainly, the day went faster and more enjoyably. Whether there was great spiritual uplift is doubtful."

I asked, "Have you ever had a sense of deep belonging in a congregation?" Esther's reply, "In a congregation? No." She then immediately equated belonging with obligation, "I joined the board because I felt I had talents to bring and had an obligation to serve that community." I asked to whom she felt obliged. "Ah, I think this is a very Jewish thing. Certain things, and it goes with the way I was raised... I have a pretty strong sense of responsibility to the Jewish community and to the Jewish people even. To raise my kids Jewish was and continues to be important to me. I mean, we still light the candles every Friday and my daughter goes to services regularly, leads services often actually. So, yes, I guess the obligation is to continue the faith." I asked if she felt that same sense of obligation to the synagogue. "Joining the board seemed an appropriate, good thing to do. I was happy to do it. There was a lot of *tsuris* (Yiddish for problems). But, there's a lot of that on any board, I suppose."

I asked Esther if she felt the same sense of obligation to other boards on which she serves. Her reply, "...the same sense? No. It's different with Judaism." I asked her to articulate the difference. She replied, "I'm not sure… I have served on lots of other boards. The obligation to Judaism is different than the obligation to my secular community. It just is. How it is, I don't know. It's just ingrained, I suppose." I asked if the obligation to the Jewish community is a positive thing in Esther's life. "It's mixed. Uh, it's certainly positive and I'm happy to do it, but you know it's a quote-unquote burden as well. It's something that one bears. For the most part, I do it happily, so I'm good with it." I asked if she could articulate what was burdensome. "Oh, it involves time, effort, sacrifice, and all that… It's almost a burden one is happy to bear, if that makes sense?"

I asked Esther whether when she is serving out of a sense of obligation to the Jewish community, she ever feels a part of something bigger than herself. She replied, definitively, "I certainly do, when I do things in the Jewish community. Again, this sort of gets back to the obligation to, you know, not break the chain, if that's the right metaphor… Yeah, I think Judaism has a tremendous amount to offer. I try to sort of stand back and look at it and it just seems like it, I mean obviously I was raised this way, so it, it just feels like a very good fit to me… The continuation of Judaism is important to me, and I certainly feel Jewish."

I asked Esther what it would look like if the "chain" were broken. "I would be unhappy. I certainly hope that my children marry Jewish and continue their following of Judaism. I would not disown them. I would still love them. I would still welcome their spouses and children. My husband was born in a mixed household and he's the only one of the kids who married Jewish. And, I think his father (my father-in-law)… I don't think he ever expressed it to him, but I think he's very happy that at least one of his kids married Jewish."

I asked Esther what came to mind when I said the word "spirituality". "I'm not sure I ever attempted to define it. For better or worse, I don't think I'm a terribly spiritual person and I don't spend a whole lot of time thinking about it, to be quite honest." After a long pause she repeated, "I don't think I'm a very spiritual person, but I think that's one of the reasons why I don't feel spiritual in synagogue. I'm not sure I feel very spiritual, hugely spiritual, anywhere. If I do, it tends to be out of doors, it tends to be in a solitary and quiet place, maybe in the company of my husband, and that's about it. So, there we are. I guess I just don't give a whole lot of thought to spirituality because it's not where my strengths lie."

I asked if she thought her parents spent time thinking about spirituality. She replied, "I had to think about it for a second, but I don't think either of them are [spiritual]… I have a feeling that this sense of obligation was very, that what I have is learned. I think that they felt the same way. I don't think that they derived a great deal of spiritual satisfaction out of belonging to a synagogue, but they felt the obligation."

I asked Esther if she could name a moment when she decided to make her current synagogue her congregational home. "It was more of a default, almost. I've always been Reform, and when we moved to the Midwest it was [the local Reform congregation], it was close to home. I mean, everything worked out well. And, I joined, certainly within weeks (if not days) of when we moved here."

I asked, other than the default Reform affiliation, were there attributes that attracted her to the congregation? Esther's immediate reply was, "I don't even consider it. I joined basically knowing it was Reform. It was large and it was close. The largeness didn't matter to me."

I pushed on attributes that distinguish this congregation from others in the community. "The same thing I like is the thing I don't like. It's a large congregation which I'm not very fond of, but I think they honestly made an effort to reach out and welcome new members. And, I thought that was very good, particularly for a large congregation. So, I certainly felt that was good. I certainly, as I said, liked the music. I think [the cantor] is wonderful. I thought that the Sunday school was quite good. It was considerably more rigorous than the Sunday school that I attended." I asked if there were any attributes that stood out as undesirable. She said it "Felt a little churchy." I asked if the synagogue of her childhood felt the same way. She said it did.

Esther is indicative of what I consider a disaffected Jewish American, and she represents a majority of synagogue members. For most of her life, she stayed affiliated with the Jewish community, but at the same time marginally so. Her sense of obligation was not only apparent but omnipresent, and sometimes overwhelming to me as the interviewer. That sense of obligation is both a blessing and curse for Esther and when speaking about it she, perhaps for the first time, recognized the incongruity of it. I see this same sense of obligation in many other active synagogue members and, as Esther highlights, it can lead to dissatisfaction and disaffiliation.

When Esther talked about being traditional, it was apparent to me (though not so to her) that she meant traditional, Classical Reform. This is an important context distinction for Esther and others like her.

Your Implicit Preference Scale

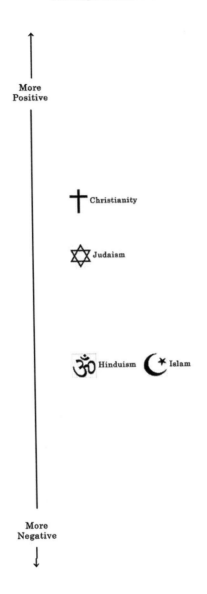

From the Society for Classical Reform Judaism's website, their goal is "...to inspire and challenge the Reform Movement – its national institutions, rabbis and congregations – to reaffirm the broad, progressive vision of the pioneers of modern liberal Judaism, who sought to renew the Jewish mission for modern times and to confidently and fully engage in the life of our American society." The tenets of this movement were articulated in the 1885 Pittsburgh Platform statement that fully distinguished Reform Judaism from Eastern European orthodoxy and created the first Jewish movement. It is distinguished by a predominance of English in worship and a formal English at that (thou, thee, whilst, etc). Services are conducted by the rabbi and music is offered by the cantor. It is clergy focused rather than participatory. There are some Classical Reform congregations, though the vast majority of Reform congregations have long moved away from this tradition.

My conversation with Esther was difficult at times. She often did not answer the questions asked, and sometimes it seemed she was offering platitudes rather than personal insights. While frustrating, I do not begrudge Esther these answers, since I got the sense she had never thought much about these issues. Rather, she served her community out of a learned or inherited sense of obligation and did what she was "supposed" to do.

Esther was clearly uncomfortable with spiritual language or anything that suggested emotional connection with God or some kind of higher, universal power. While not uncommon with other interviewees, Esther seemed to show particular discomfort with anything but intellectual discourse.

While other interviewees showed some interest in their own sense of obligation towards Judaism and the possible incongruence this might indicate, Esther seemed fully at ease with this obligation, even after acknowledging that it might not be inherited as much as implicitly expected. Though not indicative of anything in particular, it is interesting to note that Esther scored Christianity higher on the IAT (Figure 3) than Judaism. If I were to suggest any meaning, it would be that she values secular over religious, equating Christianity with secular culture versus Judaism with religion.

Marcie

Marcie is a 40-65 year old woman, considers herself Reform and is a member of two synagogues (both Reform), though her membership in the second is very recent. All of her answers were based on history with the synagogue with which she had the longest affiliation. She is a regular worship attendee and active in leadership in her community. While Marcie grew up in the same city where she now lives, she is not a member of the Conservative synagogue of her childhood. Her parents were both Holocaust survivors and her father was a well-known Holocaust speaker. Marcie's extended family is also known in the community for this legacy.

I asked Marcie to name a positive synagogue experience. Her immediate reply was her first child's *bris*.[50] I asked why it was positive. "Ah, you know, following the covenant, the long tradition." I asked if she felt connected to something when it was happening, and, if so, what it might be. She answered, "Um, ah, I don't know what you mean by something, but the whole thing just felt good, just the whole memory of it. I don't know... I can't say. You know, the whole thing just felt really good. Actually connected to anything... you know, if you think of connected to something, because of God I can't say he has no, um, the... Just the covenant part of that tradition that um, ah, you know, I remember that by time. I can remember, you know, my father-in-law holding him. Everybody being there, ah, in general it just felt good. I don't know about the... connection with other people and family." If Marcie's answer seems unintelligible, it was. She started off having a very difficult time connecting historical actions or events with feelings, or any sense of relationship or correlation to something else.

I pressed her to see if she could verbalize what felt good, and what that good feeling was really about. "... specifically that my son, being from my father who is a [Holocaust] survivor... the turmoil that they had to go through to... through the Holocaust, for my dad to be a survivor. To show that you're still, you're still Jewish, you're still here...kinda like 'in your face, we're still here, we survived'."

Without prompting, Marcie continued. "When [son] was about *bar mitzvah* age, before he actually even started [*bar mitzvah* training], he was complaining about not wanting to do it and, actually, I'm explaining to him, 'look what your father, what your grandfather had to go through. There is no way that you are not going to go do this.' And, I said, 'you'll understand. But, it's something that your

---

[50] She was referring to the *b'rith milah* ceremony, often referred to as *bris*, ritual circumcision.

43

grandparents gave their lives, your aunt, your uncle, because they were killed just because of the... and, and you're going to go ahead and have a *bar mitzvah*'. You know, during the year, obviously he switched his mind and got up in front of people, but that's where actually I had to explain that 'you know, your family passed, there is no way you're not going to do it.'" I asked if it worked – if her son followed through by choice or by coercion. "It worked, and obviously if you knew my kid, he went from not wanting [a *bar mitzvah*] to being extremely active [in the Jewish community], and still is to this day."

I asked if Marcie could name a time when she felt alive, enthused, excited about her synagogue. "I still have to go back to what I've already mentioned, my son's *bris*, my son's *bar mitzvah*, my daughter's *bat mitzvah*. There were some issues politically at the time on some of them. Like my daughter's *bat mitzvah*, when there was a rabbi switch. But, it was also the anniversary of the congregation and [a former senior rabbi] came back, and so it's kind of neat to have him back there for that. But, I think part of feeling connected at that point is also the fact that you're so happy about what's happening with the event itself. I don't know if that was [because of] the congregation as much it was just the fact that my kids were going through one of the major events in their lives."

I remarked that this was a good distinction, the event from the event in this synagogue. I asked if she thought she might have felt the same if they happened in another place. "If it would have been a different congregation, yeah I think I still would have been fond of it. I don't think the congregation itself would have made any difference in that perspective."

I then asked Marcie if she could name an experience when she felt a deep sense of belonging in the synagogue. She replied, "I can do that in a positive and in a negative way. I left [the synagogue of my youth] to go to [my current synagogue] because my husband was part of the latter and he wanted something that was our own. But, I also felt I had a belonging [to the synagogue of my youth], that I felt torn because I didn't get along with the rabbi that well and my sense of belonging was a sense of almost being pushed out of my home... I have to say that I had a similar feeling recently, things that were happening at my synagogue when I was on the board, and there was a rabbi change, and I saw things politically happening in a place that I didn't think should have been happening, and my sense of belonging was violated. I still feel like I belong there. Sometimes, there are certain aspects that make you cringe. But, you know, as I look at it from the positive point of view, being sisterhood president, when I'm with the sisterhood, you feel the sense of belonging with the gals, that you have that camaraderie. And, that there we keep the other part of it [politics] out and that when the gals are together, then it's the sisterhood. Yeah. I feel that sense of belonging in that way, in a positive way without being negative at all. We feel like we're doing good things. We do good things for education, to get the kids to want to be Jewish and to grow. So, yeah, that's the place where I can totally be positive. You know, making *latkes*[51], doing the *Purim* lunch. It's good."

I asked when in this positive mode, did she feel part of something bigger. "Sometimes. Yeah. Especially when the other ladies are getting together and it's working, and you get participation, definitely. Then it does feel that it's bigger than I am, and that gives you a good feeling." I asked what that "bigger than yourself" would be; to describe or name it. "If I were to guess, the feeling you get is when you're doing something and it involves a larger group, and it can feel like family, and you know the things you're doing are good, and you know the people participating; you get that same feeling when you're with family and friends. [It's a] very friendly feeling. Let's put it that way. That's when it feels good, and that's a way I guess I could think of it even if they're not truly an actual relation, family relation. You're there with them and they still feel like they're family."

I asked, "Would that something be having a connection to God, higher power, spiritual sense, whatever you want to call it?" After a long pause, she remarked, "When you actually bring God into it… it's that unknown. I want to believe there's something there, and that I am doing good things, and that the people who do bad things are going to get what they deserve later on. You know, I guess that believing in God is like believing that your father is going to find out what you did. You know, you could be bad, but there's a reason why he's trying to stay on a good path, and it's got to be because you've got to have some belief that there is something that's going to happen after you're gone, and that there is someone to judge you, and say, 'I know you're not perfect but you weren't horrible.' I guess this is kind of what I look at it. I mean, do I say things and promise things and if something turns out certainly, yeah, I guess I do, but do I have an exact image of somebody sitting on a throne or something? Not necessarily."

I asked Marcie what comes to mind when I say the word "spirituality". "Well, I think it's different things. I think of services, you know, brain form of prayer. You'd think our [Jews] specialty is going to services and the certain demeanor; the way you act. And, then there is the majority of the way you act. How you are to other people, how you treat people. There should be a certain,

---

[51] Potato pancakes traditionally served during Hanukkah.

without getting too mushy, type of spirituality, and then you have to think that there's a reason to be a decent person, that type of spirituality."

Me: "So, there's a spirituality of being a good person?"

Marcie: "Yeah. I think it goes with that, back to how you're going to be judged afterwards and if that's what you think. You can't separate the two. I mean if, you know, I'm just good in services and pray and then screw everybody over at work and cheat people... they have to coincide. There has to be a connection ...You know, I'm going to treat people decently because I want my whole life to be that way and, I mean, I can't say I'm perfect, I'm not... but they gotta connect."

I asked Marcie if she found services spiritual. "Sometimes... depends on the service." She described visiting the Jewish camp where her kids went in the summer and not knowing the songs, and not finding the services there comfortable or connecting. She shared, "Sometimes I like the old traditional prayers. Just let me do those. If it gets too modern... I'm not too wowed by guitars. Okay, but if you start changing too many tunes on me and make it feel like I'm back at school, and I have to learn every prayer or every old prayer over the new tune, you take away from my service and then I don't feel so spiritual."

Me: "So, part of what connects for you is what you know and what you're used to."

Marcie: "Yes. I'll say that. I don't want to say I won't learn anything new, but sometimes it's just too much new and not enough tradition."

Me: "Are there other things that you would consider spiritual?"

Marcie: "... ah, I don't go looking for a whole lot of deep meaning in things. I don't really search for it. If it happens and it feels good and, yeah, I might say that. If you ask me that moment, I might say yes. That's about that."

I asked if there was something spiritual in her childhood and if her parents ever talked about God. She shared that while her life centered around the Jewish community and other Jews, it was community in the secular sense not the religious. She said her life was "geared around being Jewish... we always knew we were Jewish."

I asked, "Can you think of a moment when you decided - any congregation in your life - that this is my home, spiritual home, Jewish home, did you ever have that sense?" Marcie replied, "Well, growing up [our family's synagogue]... I mean, I was there from day one. It always felt like my home and that. When I left,

46

I felt like I was leaving my home… It [the transition to the Reform congregation] was kind of gradual. I can't say there's an exact time, but there was a point where I did think to myself that it finally feels like home. And, I still kind of feel like it's my home sometimes, but yet with all the turmoil, with the last rabbi being removed or not rehired, I should say it felt like there was an intruder in the home. And, being part of the new congregation [new Reform synagogue], it's nice, but I can't say it feels like home per say yet, cuz it doesn't have a location to be a home. You can have family but not have a home. And, it doesn't feel like there's a home yet."

I asked Marcie if she could identify the attributes that attracted her to the synagogue of her adulthood. She reiterated that she had not picked the synagogue as much as chose to leave the synagogue of her childhood because her husband did not feel comfortable there. She went on to say, "I'm not sure that [has] always been the best idea. And, if it weren't for my feeling towards the rabbis at the time, I don't know if I wouldn't have pulled him back to [synagogue of childhood]… eventually I made it feel like it was my place to be, and then as I got more [involved] with the activities there, that made it feel more and more like it was my place. The more active I thought, the more I participated, that's what made it feel like it was a home, working with sisterhood, doing just that kind of stuff."

Me: "So, it was probably less an intentional choosing of [current synagogue] and more that the options in this community were limited?"

Marcie: "My husband grew up Reform and I felt I had to have the connection with something. And, that my husband wanted to be there, and I felt very comfortable with the [rabbi at the time), and because he was there, it made it fairly easy to say, 'okay, I'll go over there'. Then, when we actually chose to be members, we had some dues issues because I was a student and wasn't making much money. Our income if anything was negative, cuz I was taking out loans and they still made me pay our regular dues. And, as mad as I was, I still wanted to be a member. Just because I wanted to, I felt like I should be part of the community, and that was it. I thought, like, I should be part of the community. I think that was instilled from my parents that you're just supposed to be part of it. Okay, what happens if I'm not? I should be, but I'm not. Are there consequences to that?"

Moving to Marcie's survey answers, she said that synagogue membership is important – not essential, but important. "On two questions, 'strong sense of belonging to the Jewish people' and 'I have many friends who are Jewish', you're as far "yes" as you can go. And, then in the question 'synagogue membership is essential to my Jewishness', you said strongly disagree." Marcie replied, "I don't think you have to be a member, it's just that guilty thing if you're not a member. But, you could do all kinds of Jewish things and not have to be a member. It's almost a guilt thing that if I'm not a member but I think I have to be a member, and politics are what would drive me away. If the politics were too much, I could easily walk away, because politics start becoming a thing to me, losing your judgment of it, and so I don't need that. I can't be Jewish without it [synagogue membership]."

I asked if she thought one could be a member of the Jewish community without membership in a synagogue. She replied, "You could be out there and be very Jewish and not be a member of a synagogue."

I asked Marcie what makes her Jewish. "I was born a Jew. That, first and foremost, automatically gave me my heritage. Not that I think people can't convert... sometimes I feel like we're burdened with it and they're choosing the burden. You kind of wonder why. Why would you choose to have the situation [of being Jewish]? Not that it isn't good, I'm proud of my heritage, but if you weren't born into it and went into it knowing everything that goes with it, it takes a strong person to pick it."

I asked Marcie to tell me how she would describe Judaism to someone who knew nothing of religion. "There's the Torah, which is the Bible, which if they have no idea what any religion is, it's still going to be hard to explain that there's stories that tell you kind of where you came from, and give you some of your heritage, and have rules in them that have been argued and changed and manipulated by whoever, our sages and rabbis, and our leaders. They've come down to certain rules, that this is the things that you should listen to, and you can pick which way you want to listen, and there are people who are more observant and less observant, but basically comes down to living your life in a good way that treats people with dignity and respect."

Me: "So, if they said, you live by a set of rules written by dead people?"

Marcie: "Ah, I would say written by ancestors which are more alive than they are dead at this point because it's been going on for thousands of years. Just cuz you're dead doesn't mean what you had to say wasn't important."

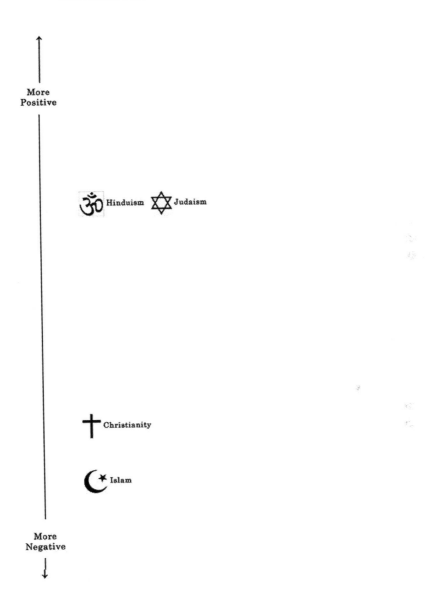

Marcie's was a frustrating interview. A successful medical professional, she is clearly an intelligent person. However, her answers rambled, digressed into other topics, and basically blathered on to seeming inconsequentiality.

If there was a theme to Marcie's relationship to her synagogue, and maybe to Judaism in general, it would easily be identified as guilt. She is clearly driven by doing the right thing in order to avoid any possible consequences. Interestingly, this is not a theological concept in Judaism, though not uncommonly perceived as one by Jewishly uneducated Jews.

In retrospect, if I had realized the influence of the Holocaust on Marcie and her family, I might not have chosen her as an interview subject. Survivors, and particularly children of survivors, have a unique, though jaundiced view of Judaism. This is certainly understandable given their family history. With this said, I think Marcie's final answer, "Just cuz you're dead doesn't mean what you had to say wasn't important," is one of the most profound of all the interviews. There is a saying in Judaism taken from the Talmud, "*mitoch shelo lishma ba lishma*", literally "for out of not for its own sake comes for its own sake." It's taken to mean that even though one does something good for the wrong reason, one will eventually do it for the right reason. I think this sums up Marcie quite nicely!

Michelle

Michelle is a member of the synagogue of her childhood. She grew up and now lives in the same city with her extended family. Interestingly, all three of her siblings who still live in town are members of this same synagogue. She is in the 40 to 65 year old age range, identifies as a Reconstructionist, and is active in other Jewish institutions. Michelle attended Hebrew and Sunday school, as well as Jewish camp, and was a member of a Jewish youth group.

Michelle could not name one outstanding positive experience with her synagogue, either as a child or an adult. However, she shared that any of the various lifecycle events of her adulthood – her marriage and the *bar/bat mitzvah's* of her children come to mind as positive experiences. When she and her husband were starting their family, the Friday night services also stood out for her as positive experiences. For Michelle, positive experience equated with family. When pressed to explain what attending Friday services with her young children felt like, she related that "I don't think I'm that much of a spiritual person. But, I think it was a communal experience, probably the singing and the feeling of community, belonging to a community that made it feel positive. And, I guess I walked out of there feeling good about being there and then heading to dinner, as a family."

I asked what belonging felt like and Michelle shared, "I don't know everybody, but it's a sense, a feeling, that it's a close community. And, that if I was in trouble, if I needed something, or whatever, I could probably, ask anyone... I wouldn't be apt to do that, but I feel as if I could." She quickly shared, "You know, I've had that similar experience, say at the, at a G.A.[52] and at a couple Jewish group meetings. There is something about it. And, I don't know if it's all religions. I don't think a lot of people have those experiences as much as Jews do, maybe, or as much as I do. But, I mean, you go to the G.A., and you feel like there's, well, a shared history and a shared bond. Even though you don't know them, there's something about knowing everybody's Jewish and that you're in that community."

Pressing on the sense of community, I asked who the "community" was when she was with her family at synagogue. She answered first, "I don't know." After some thought, she came up with "I guess it's a caring about each other; that there's some shared caring for each other that I don't think I have generally walking down the street. I don't think in a store, let's say, I don't feel that same connection to the others that they care about me and that I care about them. But, I

---

[52] General Assembly, Jewish Federations of North America annual meeting.

think at the synagogue and in that community, I feel as if there's something like that, that both sides care about the other." She then quickly related that she experiences this sense in almost any Jewish gathering and in Israel "where I know it's all Jewish people around me."

When I asked about experiences in synagogue that left Michelle feeling alive or uplifted, again she was unable to think of specific instances. She did share that uplifting music (as opposed to the same rote melodies) gave her this sense of uplift. "It's not as though I mind the prayers... I like when there's an interjection of something different." She equated sameness of melody with something impersonal. When I asked what makes worship services personal for her, she shared that when things are changed around, occasionally it seems "tailored towards me, or that day, or that period... there was something that identified the day and the time in history, and we weren't doing the exact same thing we did the week before."

I asked what makes a service alive. Michelle said, "Where you feel the energy of everybody there. Usually, I think all rabbis do a good job, whether it's starting out with a few songs that are more lively, that get people involved, that there's an energy feeling, and I think that brings people alive as opposed to a synagogue where you start out with one song and you start reading the Hebrew and the prayers, and it's just so repetitive. It doesn't feel as if there's any energy behind it." When I pressed her to articulate the difference between people singing something that is new and alive and something that is old and repetitive she said, "Yeah, most of the time I think it deals with leadership." She recounted her experience of attending worship at another synagogue where it seemed the rabbi lacked enthusiasm and excitement about the worship experience. "Let sing it, let's get it over." When the rabbi at her synagogue leads worship she said, "I think he gets people... it feels energetic, he puts some energy behind it. I think because he puts the energy behind it, the congregation does. At the other synagogue... I don't think that happened. I think the rabbi or the cantor was doing it because they had to do it, not because they wanted to do it. And, that came through."

I asked Michelle to help me understand better why worship leadership was so important to her. "We're all here to celebrate, not just here to pray. Just because it's Friday night, and we're supposed to be here. Let's celebrate the end of the week and the wonders of *Shabbat* as opposed to just another day and another service. I see that come through a lot wherever I go, wherever you see a rabbi leading the service. You can tell the ones who it's a job for or it's part... where it's just a job, or they're putting their all into it."

When I asked about belonging, Michelle was ambivalent. Even though she grew up in the synagogue and raised her own family in the same congregation, she still sometimes feels like she does not belong. She shared that she and her husband have often talked about seeking an alternative synagogue community and have even explored the alternatives. The lack of viable options has made their current affiliation their default choice. Similarly, when asked if she feels a part of something bigger than herself, she quickly answered, "Yes, but not at this synagogue." Her sense of belonging and connection comes from other places, like attending large Jewish conferences and traveling to Poland, Hungary and Israel. During the trips to Eastern Europe, it was the sense that her family came from this land, and she expressed a deep sense of loss visiting Auschwitz and other Holocaust sites.

I asked Michelle to define and describe spirituality. She responded, "I envy people who have that. I mean, I wish I did. But, I don't. How do you describe it? I guess because I never had it, it's hard to describe." She really seemed to struggle with the term and concept, and believes it is something missing in her life. When I asked if she considered her experience at Auschwitz a spiritual experience, she paused, then answered "... maybe it was... I don't know. At the time, I didn't think so. I'm not sure I thought, spiritual didn't come to mind. But, it moved me."

Since she described a sense of connectedness during worship, I asked if being part of the community might be a spiritual experience. "I guess it could be. I don't know. I've never allowed it to be. I don't know why I separate them. I don't know why I think of spirituality as the connection with God, or a higher being, or something like that as opposed to community? I don't know?"

I asked if her parents or grandparents ever talked about God or spirituality. Her answer was clearly no, though in the same sentence she recounted that whenever her grandfather came to visit they always went to daily *minyan* and *Shabbat* services.

When asked if Michelle ever made a conscious decision to make her current synagogue her home (as opposed to it being her parents'), she answered no. She recounted a bad experience with the rabbi that, in her words, led to her oldest son shying away from Judaism. Continuing her critique, she shared, "I'm not sure (the) synagogue has done all they should and could do to attract families and try and improve things. I think they're content with how they are. And, I don't think the cantor is what we need to bring young people there." And, following this critique she shared, "While I say all that stuff, I think there are things that the rabbis do right. And, I guess things haven't been bad enough to push us away. But, it probably wouldn't take too much if there were good alternatives. But, I don't feel comfortable with the Reform service. I didn't like the previous Conservative rabbi [at another congregation] even though it [another synagogue] was real close to our house. I don't know much about the new one [new synagogue in the area], but it's just too far and we wouldn't go. So, we don't have alternatives."

On the survey, Michelle shared that she was unsure if synagogue membership is important to Jewishness. When we discussed this, she somewhat retracted her answer and said that it is important, but her answer is colored by her personal experience. I asked if it is more important to tolerate the downsides of her current affiliation than to be unaffiliated. "I think it's important to have a home synagogue. I think it's somewhat grounding, for me at least. I can see everybody can be different. I'm not saying it's for everybody. But, I think it's important to be a member of a synagogue." I asked what grounded meant to her. "I think I feel that it's having that platform sort of, for the Jewish practice, for the holidays, all the life cycle events, and I'm not sure what we'd do if we weren't members of a synagogue… I guess my grounding is that it's that base, baseline for the Jewish life cycle events that you need the synagogue." I asked if there would still be that connectedness if she could get those services outside the synagogue. She answered, "Not necessarily… being a member of the synagogue gives me easy access to things that I might need at some point in my life, or being a member of a synagogue is essential to being a Jew. I don't think that it's essential for everybody for that, but I think that I'd still be Jewish without it. But, I think it's knowing that there's that place for me; and having that there is definitely not the essence of Judaism, but it's important."

I asked Michelle what Jewishness meant to her. She answered that it was the practice of Judaism and being Jewish. I pressed her to make a distinction between practicing and being. She had a difficult time deciding which was Jewishness – the practice of Judaism or being Jewish. She agreed that one did not have to practice Judaism to be Jewish. Regarding the synagogue, she also shared that "…it doesn't make you Jewish just to join… you can join and never step foot inside and still be Jewish… be doing things at home. But, I don't think you can only pay your dues and say that's my Judaism. They can treat people poorly and do all the things against Judaism and do nothing else Jewish in your life, though I understand you could be born Jewish and that's the end of it. But, I wouldn't count myself just much of a Jew if I just paid my membership and lived the total secular life… But, I can definitely see how I'm that way. I pick and choose what Judaism that I want,

54

what Jewishness I want, and I see how there are lots of people in that spectrum, but if it's just membership, if the only thing is membership in a synagogue, then that doesn't do it for me."

Michelle was on the synagogue's board at one time. She shared that it was not a positive experience, primarily because she felt that she had no say. She said the board made no substantive decisions. Those were made by an executive committee. I asked if there was anything that felt Jewish about being on the board. "No, actually, I always thought that was a little bit strange. I mean, there were a number of people I'd never seen before in my life which I always thought was kinda, you know, odd. We don't go that often anymore, but then we were going often and it just always struck me as strange when the leadership, especially the executive committee, they were going because they have to be on the *bima*[53] and everything... But, they aren't regulars, and I always found that kinda strange because I look at other organizations, and usually, it's people involved more before they get on the board and before they do that, you sort of earn your place on the board." I asked Michelle if, as a member of the synagogue she felt like a stakeholder. Her prompt reply was no.

My final question was, "What makes you Jewish?" After a lengthy pause and several uh's, she answered, "I guess I want to believe my belief system. I guess because my education got me there, but I'd say my belief system makes me Jewish, what I believe in. I don't think about that but every once in a while. I can't believe another religion is that far, that much different in terms of the core beliefs. But, if I had to say, I'd say my belief system is Jewish. I think when I think about what I've learned about Judaism, I agree with most of it." When asked how she would describe Judaism to someone who knew nothing about religion, she started with the pat answer of belief in one God. Then she caught herself and shared that she is not sure she even believes in God, so that would be a poor answer. It took some teasing out, but she finally shared, "I believe in doing what I've been taught is right. And, you know, doing unto others what I'd have them do unto me. What I think is a peace-loving, caring religion that will do nothing detrimental to others; a humane way of living."

I found Michelle to be intelligent and very sincere about her answers. However, it was clear that these were questions she had never been asked or asked herself. I could see that many, especially those about spirituality were difficult, even painful for her to articulate. It was clear that Judaism is important to her, but in many respects she does not know why.

---

[53] Platform in synagogue, usually at the front on which the ark sits.

Your Implicit Preference Scale

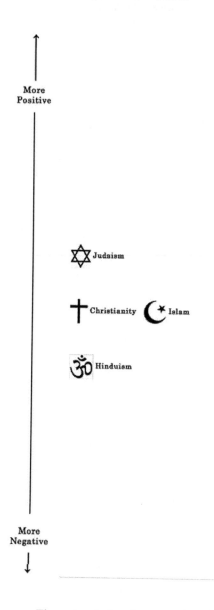

There is obviously a tension between her family's current synagogue affiliation and her search for something meaningful. She seemed resigned to the fact that she would not find what she is looking for in her synagogue community.

She also seems to have made the decision that she is not spiritual even when presented with contrary evidence. Without psychologizing, Michelle, like many Jews, believes that spirituality is only God-focused and connection to community and history play no part.

It was difficult to find cues in Michelle's interview. Her affect was monotone and unemotional, even while criticizing her own synagogue and articulating her apparent double standard regarding her own synagogue. However, I did notice times of increased discomfort when I asked about spirituality. It was apparent that Michelle is interested, dare I say searching, for something meaningful in her faith community. Several times there was incongruity in her language, for instance relating Judaism as a way of being and then describing its practice. Sometimes, she caught herself on these incongruities; several times, I called her on them and she readily admitted her lack of clarity.

It was clear to me that Michelle finds community and connection first with family and with Jews. I did not get the sense that she feels this in exclusion of other religions, though she did score Judaism higher on the IAT than any other religion (Figure 5). Interestingly, Judaism falls at the midpoint of the IAT scale instead of at the top. Seemingly, although Michelle puts high value in connection to other Jews, Judaism as a religion is less valuable.

The takeaways from Michelle are her deep sense of commitment to Jewish community. I sensed this was less a feeling of obligation than a deeply rooted commitment to a sense of community ownership. She seems to seek relationships with other Jews and finds avenues for these relationships in her work with Jewish communal institutions. Unfortunately, synagogue does not play prominently in this sense of ownership, though it was clear that if she had other alternatives to explore she might find this at another synagogue. In a metaphorical way, Michelle is looking for a personal connection between synagogue and herself. Unfortunately, it appears to be in a congregation that is impersonal and does not foster connectedness. Michelle described community and family as interconnected.

Sam

Sam identifies as a Reform Jew and is in the 26 to 39 year old age group. He is married with three young children. He and his wife are not natives of their current city of residence, though they grew up in the same state. It is notable that Sam worked as a Jewish professional until his wife became pregnant with their first child. After a several year hiatus, he is returning to a role as a professional Jewish communal leader. He and his family are members of a Reform synagogue.

I asked Sam to name a positive synagogue experience. He shared that "thankfully, I've had several," but the one that came first to mind: "I experienced *Simchat Torah*[54] with my five-year-old and three-year-old daughters, and for the first time, really, really enjoyed the celebration. It really felt a party, and great to see several dozens of kids running around with little stuffed Torahs. It was really a neat way that [rabbi of the congregation] did it this year. He had two Torahs, and he had one rolled to the end and one rolled to the beginning, each one held by two people, and he had invited three or four or five congregants to have different parts to read that they had prepared, and (not knowing) how this is going to work, and I really want my kids to see what I remember this feeling like [when he was a child] …So, it just totally came alive for my five-year-old. It made complete sense to see one scroll, huge, and little, and little, and huge to really understand, and then it felt like a party. He understood that we are celebrating the Torah. So, that was a lot of fun." I asked if he could identify what made this a positive experience.

Sam: "I have three children, 5, 3 and 1, and engaging with Judaism as a parent has been very rewarding. So, I think that seeing holidays and celebrations through their eyes is just fun."

Me: "So, it might not have been as powerful if you didn't have kids?"

Sam: "No, it would not have been as powerful if I did not have my kids. I like to think that I would have still gotten a kick out of it, but I probably, I may not have been there, you know? I wasn't really paying attention to what older congregants without kids were doing cuz it was kind of crazy, you know, running around. So, yeah."

I asked if he could name an experience when he felt enthused, fulfilled, or alive in the synagogue that did not involve experiencing through his children. "You know, once a month (our synagogue) we're now doing a spiritual Shabbat,

---

[54] Jewish holiday celebrating the giving of the Torah at Mt. Sinai.

and those have been really wonderful. Specifically, with respect to those services, we have started a program, maybe a couple of months in, to offer; children between the ages of, like, 3 or 7 or 8 are invited to leave. The idea being that they can have their holy time, but parents also need their holy time. And, we can expect some decorum from them. We can expect them to sit for 10 or 15 minutes and know to stay and be part of the service and then have their own program, and it might be coloring or story or game. It's not too rigorous, but there is something about the feeling I have when they leave the sanctuary, where I get to sit alone and actually just listen and just focus. You know, 9 times out of 10, I'm moved by what (rabbi) has to share and then at that service, he does a lot of the writings. I think he just might have a knack for prayer, writing prayer, poems, and I really enjoy it… and to listen to a sermon, you know, undistracted. And, to be excited and then to be excited when they [the kids] come back. I've had a half hour of an experience for myself and, when they come back in at the end, have a little bit of a renewed energy, because I was just able to experience a little bit of Shabbat just for myself."

Continuing the theme, I asked what is moving for him about the experience. "… just sort of to stop, to really just stop, to let something resonate that I might hear and enjoy music for a minute… to not be busy in my head, to find quiet for myself for a few minutes."

I asked if Sam experiences moments like this in other parts of his life. "I'm moved when I watch my children sometimes. You have those moments where, you know, you stop and say 'these three amazing kids that are totally crazy but totally wonderful and infuriated me two seconds ago, and yet I'm madly in love with them now'. And, so I try and stop and appreciate those, those moments."

I asked if Sam felt a sense of belonging to/in his synagogue. He replied, "I do." I asked if he had that sense when he was a child. "I did." I followed with asking if he could identify what that felt like when he was a child. "I felt like I knew the physical space of the synagogue, the temple. I knew certain faces that I would see. I am the third of three children, and my two older sisters are 5 and 7 years older than me, so they're like 18 months apart. And so, from 6th grade on, I was an only child; they were all in college already. So, getting ready for my *bar mitzvah*, that's high school, or even younger when I was in 3rd to 4th grade, they were in high school doing stuff and I was going to temple. So, I don't remember being at temple that much with my sisters, but I remember going regularly. In the mid-80s, my dad was president of the temple. My mom was the assistant president, so they were there obviously very involved."

I asked if as an adult he had the same sense of belonging as when he was young. "...yeah. I mean, this is a bigger congregation. The congregation I grew up in had maybe 300 families or 350, so there's more faces [in his current congregation], so I'm not familiar with all of them by any means. But, then I served on the board of directors. I did a 3 year term which ended about 6 months ago and I'm active in the early childhood center. And, that was one of the biggest reasons for me to have my kids going to the preschool here, because I wanted them to be walking into the synagogue as much as possible and be familiar with the faces, from the clergy to the janitorial staff. If (daughter's names) need to go someplace, I can tell them, 'go, you know where it is, you know where the drinking fountain is'. And, they feel comfortable doing that."

I asked, "So, belonging for you has a real physical component?" He replied, "Oh yeah, I think so."

I asked Sam if he could translate that sense of comfort into being part of something bigger than himself. "There's definitely the immediate family aspect of it. But, I'm a firm believer that I'm as connected to the Jewish community as I am because of the role model of my parents, and this is to Israel and Jewish camp, and all of that. If I'm going to do the same thing for my kids, then I need to set that example for them. So, I guess that was immediate comfort of just my family feeling good in the synagogue, but I also feel like it's an example that I am setting for not just my kids, but my kid's kids. So, there's that impact. And, then I think that there are things that I feel a part of, you know, socially, politically, professionally. When I was working for the (local Jewish agency), I participated in a march for (Jewish cause) in 2003 in [Washington,] DC. And, that was an experience where I really felt like I was part of something bigger."

I asked if that something bigger included something spiritual like God, a higher power, etc. "I could probably find a way... ah, I mean, there is something connecting me to God through all these things. I mean, all the things I feel connected to. Really connected to... that I would travel for that, I would donate to that, I would try to set an example. So, eventually, I could eventually connect that to... a relationship with God, but I think it's more about a relationship with Judaism and the Jewish people, and Jewish history, and a Jewish future, than it is about my relationship with God."

I asked him what comes to mind when he hears the word "spirituality". "Um... it floats. It seemed like a really great word maybe 10 years ago, and now maybe it's a little overused, but still appropriate. I think in Israel you are either religious or you're not religious. They have a hard time conceptualizing this idea of, well, what are... you're either observant or you're not. You're religious or you're not. And, that obviously doesn't exist here. So, to come up with another word to say, 'listen, I'm engaging with my religion and not observing everything that another person might be,' and so maybe the word is spiritual."

I asked, "Are there things that you consider spiritual or whatever words that you want to use?" He replied, "Um, yeah. Yeah. I think that I could... put the word spiritual on those kinds of (things). I'm one of those people who like to say (and usually believe) that decisions, things that seem like big decisions, can usually be made, *are* usually made for you. Like, something becomes evident. So, being open to whatever that development is can potentially be a spiritual moment. And, I go back to being a parent in the last three months where my family dealt with three deaths – a family member, an old friend and a community member – and I've had to sort of engage with my 5 year old about (one of those). That was my grandmother, (her) great grandmother. And, every 10 or 12 days or so (and it's been almost 2 months since she passed away), my 5 year old will say something to me about her, just sort of out of nowhere, and we find ourselves engaged in a three minute, very deep philosophical conversation that as a parent, I sort of have to jump in, focus, figure out what I want to say, or let her feel, about death and dying, and then be able to move on again when she is ready to talk about sparkly stickers."

I asked Sam if he thought his upbringing had a spiritual component. "There were certain customs, certain traditions, but it didn't really feel that spiritual." I asked if his parents ever talked about God or things spiritual. "I think the first time I really engaged with this, an idea of God... I don't remember it really being with respect to my parents. I was in my confirmation class and I wrote... I don't even remember what the assignment was, but all I know is that, to fulfill the assignment, I wrote a *midrash*[55] on the 3rd or 4th day in Genesis. Whatever verse that it would be. And, it was really fun to engage with the text. It was fun to just make up a story and say, 'well, this is what I think', and to have it be sort of valid cuz it's on the rush and I can say whatever. And, to engage with the text without thinking about whether it was true or not, really happened or not. Whether God really existed or not, it was just 'what else can I say about what might have happened in the story and what that might mean for me, and then not for anybody else?' So, I remember feeling sort of proud of an original idea. You don't have that many in your life. And, that being acknowledged by my rabbi. So, that was

---

[55] Textual interpretation.

significant. I went to Israel several times, and I haven't really had the spiritual experiences where I should have like the Western Wall, Sfat[56]... there weren't specific, spiritual connections to God... I (wasn't really) looking for that."

I asked Sam if he could name the moment or time when he decided his current synagogue was his home congregation. "I've just felt very connected to Reform Judaism. So, if there were several viable Reform congregations, then it would be a decision about which Reform congregation. But, I think there was a time right when we moved here as adults where we went to a couple of services at [another synagogue] and I certainly remember being impressed by (the rabbi) and I enjoyed it, but I'm a Reform Jew."

I asked, then, if it was his synagogue experience as a child that informed his Reform Judaism allegiance. "I'd say Jewish camping was a huge part of it, and youth group. That music, the (Reform) liturgy, that approach. My undergraduate degree is in Jewish Studies and history, and my graduate degree is in history, and I did the history of Jewish education for my Master's thesis, and a (Jewish) history of a Midwest city. So, engaging with Jewish history, I think that I've always just rooted for Reform Judaism. Well, maybe not rooted for it, but just like I maybe root for Democrats. Like there's something at its core, and it's in its core that I really believe that maybe I have something I completely appreciate." He went on to illustrate his appreciation for the role and history of other Jewish movements.

I asked if Sam could name some attributes of his synagogue that he does not like. "I'm progressive. This is my experience, and I know that there are congregants who might not be having the same experience. But, there is a path, a goal, and it feels like we're all sort of getting on it. So, we're becoming more connected. We're becoming warmer. We're becoming more interesting. I mean, I'm more engaged intellectually in Judaism than I've been in a long time, which is great. I'm inspired, thankfully, and I have confidence in our leadership. It feels like a good time right now, so that's good."

I asked, "What does inspired look like for you?" "Inspired is a combination of feeling like I'm learning something. Feeling like I can be hopeful for something. Feeling like I'm working towards something (that) is worthwhile and not just necessary. Feeling connected, feeling led, trusting leadership. I had an interaction very soon after (current rabbi) came. Here we are in the middle of June, he officially started July 1[57]. Everything was starting to happen. It was, like, July 8th

---

[56] City in Israel, also known as Safed considered one of Israel's holy cities
[57] The current senior rabbi was hired as an associate rabbi before the board decided not to renew senior rabbi's contract.

that (former rabbi's) contract was not renewed, so this was, like, September maybe. The high holidays (were coming) and I had been asked to see if we could get tot Shabbat (young children focused) going again, and I had sent out an e-mail, and I had copied the president (and) the ECC director. I had copied like 6 or 7 people, including the rabbi, including the cantor, and with the whole laundry list of 'is anybody following up on this? And, what about this? And, can we get dates?' And, I didn't hear back from anybody. And, I was walking out of temple one morning and (current rabbi) was walking in, and he's shouldering it all at this point, and been thrown in, and he said 'thank you for your e-mail. Thank you for all your work.' I said, 'yeah, well, you know, I want to make sure this works'. And he said, 'you don't need to copy all those people. We can have a conversation about this and see where these things go.' And I said, 'okay, I just want to make sure…' and he said, 'yeah, I want you to hear me; next time, come talk to me.' And, I stopped for a minute and I thought, 'oh my God, he's a leader' [laugh]. He's right. I don't need to copy 15 people and have a public conversation about something. I can have one conversation, and know and trust that it's going to move forward and other people will be involved as they need to be, but I don't need to make sure everybody knows that I have copied the rabbi on it. I was sort of, for a second, I was a little like, 'excuse me?'. You know, a little put in my place and then I thought 'oh my gosh, that's great'. Put me in my place, tell me. Lead this congregation one congregant at a time. And, if I am one, so be it. And, I saluted him and said 'point taken, very good', and I appreciated that and it really stuck with me."

I again asked if there are any attributes of the synagogue he does not like. "Well, it would be nice if everybody was involved, and I mean everybody. I don't know if it's about this congregation or if it's about everybody, but something I took from my dad, cuz my dad was temple president and a Federation president, and my sister is the Federation Executive. And, so I've heard solicitation stories and I've heard relationship stories, and him as a leader, and you hear those things when it's in your family… that my dad and my sister never had the patience for people who hold grudges and take it out on a synagogue or on the Federation. That's just ridiculous, so when I hear stories like that, that just seems so short sighted and so petty, and so those things happen. There is major stress in the congregation, and it happens to every congregation over and over and over again. That's impossible not to happen to me. That's how a community sort of grows or changes or turns a corner, but for people who feel slighted or to really hold that anger, I just don't have a lot of patience or respect for it. For people who don't feel like they're being heard or don't feel like they've been generally connected, and are willing to engage in trying to improve, I'm willing to listen all day long. But, for people who are pissed and all ready to walk away and then talk about it, I don't have patience for that."

Sam's survey answers about synagogue importance and synagogue as central to his Jewish life were congruent. He answered that both were very important. I asked what about being part of a synagogue is most important to him. "I think that's where you engage with the cycle of holidays and events. There is an ebb and flow. There's a calendar, there are preparations, looking ahead (at) what's coming next. How are we going to interface with this holiday or this *Shabbat* or this *seder*? How am I going to educate my children? How am I going to deal with grief? It's the first place I go for community in the Jewish community. I feel very strongly about the role of Federation and I think that Jews connecting to each other, and to Israel, and to Jewish communities around the world regardless of denomination, is very important. Finding that sort of central hub where I can connect with Jews that aren't just Reform Jews. But, when I'm engaging with loss or birth or, you know, something like that... you know, (my wife) and I felt very strongly that for each of our kids we did a baby naming. Certainly, we did one in our home and we did one in our (family's) home up in (other city), and we did one in the synagogue because if we're a member of a congregation and we want the community to feel connected to us, we have to let the community connect to our family's life cycle events. So, with each child we stood on the *bimah* and had the naming ceremony. I cut and pasted from several different books where I invited cousins and nieces and aunts and uncles, and we all participated and had a very nice (event) in our home. But, when you're standing on the *bimah* and you have a rabbi participating (with) the entire congregation witnessing that event, I just think that's important." I asked if he thought he could not manage that ebb and flow by himself. He said he could, but this is "engaging as a community. Even Jews who don't come but maybe twice a year, I would presume maybe they could be engaged on a personal level. I can't imagine Judaism without community."

Sam shared that his leadership experience for his congregation was a positive experience. I asked him if he could name what was a positive for him. "Positive experience is having faith in leadership. Feeling like meetings are productive. Feeling like my thoughts or concerns, or the way I participate, is appreciated. Somewhere between, you don't want to be just the rubber stamp, but you don't want to be dumped with all of the work, and I feel like there was a pretty good balance there. To be part of the board at that (tumultuous) time in the congregation's history, I'm just glad that I know that what went on (at least from my vantage point, I wasn't in executive committee meetings), that what went on in meetings and discussions was kosher and was deliberate and there was a process. And, I really respected that. I was probably the youngest member on the board, and I served on the board with fraternity brothers of my father who got a kick out of it. I'm sure that both these gentleman got a kick out of that, 'we're on the board with (his father's name)'s son.' But, I think there is something about working with that generation, that I really appreciated being able to watch how people who have been lay leaders for 30 plus years deal with hiring an associate (rabbi), renewing contracts and search processes, building campaigns, major stuff that was going on. And, the amount of work that a lot of people did. I have a lot of respect for them, and I was glad to watch that sort of unfold and to make some mental notes. Someday, I could be a leader in that position and you just have to say what you need to say. I respected that."

Me: "Did you feel valued?"

Sam: "Yes."

Me: "How did you know you were valued?"

Sam: "I could feel it. When I would participate in meetings, I was treated respectfully. I had nice relationships with board members. I think even (after) coming off the board, it's nice seeing board members now and realizing how much I miss engaging with them, even if it was just from across the table for two hours once a month."

Me: "What makes you Jewish?"

Sam: "My history. My ancestors. My future generations. I don't like saying a struggle. When I participated in the March of the Living[58], I was a senior in high school; this is the trip to Poland and I was the only one in my high school. I was the only one in (his hometown), and so there were these huge contingency meetings, and there's this huge binder of materials, and they were meeting monthly, and I had to sort of go through that on my own. I remember sitting in the hotel lobby in Warsaw somewhere and we're just drenched with Holocaust. I mean, that's where you're living it all the time, and this person said (to the group),

---

[58] From www.motl.org, THE MARCH OF THE LIVING is an international, educational program that brings Jewish teens from all over the world to Poland on Yom Hashoah, Holocaust Memorial Day, to march from Auschwitz to Birkenau, the largest concentration camp complex built during World War II, and then to Israel to observe Yom HaZikaron, Israel Memorial Day, and Yom Ha'Atzmaut, Israel Independence Day. The goal of the March of the Living is for these young people to learn the lessons of the Holocaust and to lead the Jewish people into the future vowing Never Again.

'You know, you are not a Jew because of the Holocaust.' And, that was sort of shocking to me because it had been very easy to say 'the whole reason why we need to learn about this is so that it doesn't happen again, and to prove Hitler wrong, and to prove to the world that we're still here'. I mean, there is very much a pride sort of machismo about this March of the Living. That's why we're here, and to have somebody say this is…"

Me: "And your answer was?"

Sam: "And, my answer was that there is a lot more. It's two sides of that coin. I mean, this is one incredibly dark book, not just chapter in Jewish history, but through Jewish study and intellectual academic interaction with Jewish history, it puts in perspective that, yes, you know the Holocaust was singular for all sorts of reasons when it happened in history, its scope, all of that. But, from its beginning, Judaism and Jews had to struggle to be Jewish and to continue to exist. And, that there have been off-shoots and developments and, you know, denominations emerged, and Jews are kicked out, and we moved, and we adapt. I just …I find that whole perseverance of how did we manage in Northern Africa? How did we manage in Europe? How did we manage change? How have we interacted with society at large to make sure that we're interacting but we're still ourselves? So, I feel like I have some sort of responsibility to that legacy, to interact with society now as a Jew and still want to be a Jew today."

Sam is a dream congregant. It is apparent that his level of commitment to Judaism and then by extension to his congregation, local community, national, and worldwide community of Jews is deep and seemingly unshakable.

I am still not totally clear about the source of said commitment. Sam clearly inherited communal commitment from his parents and I do not doubt its veracity. However, it is not clear that this authentic dedication is rooted in fear, cultural pride, or some other attribute. It is interesting that when I asked him what makes him Jewish, one of his first comments was, "I don't like saying a struggle." And, then he proceeded to talk about historical Jewish struggle. There seems an incongruence of feelings versus perception regarding historical Judaism and future Judaism. As much as Sam and those like him believe they are charting a new future for Judaism, they seem stuck by past events.

I have no doubt that Sam's commitment is a lasting one. He has created his personal and professional life to center around Jewish communal service. I wonder, though, if what Sam has is transferrable to other Jews, other than his own children.

Sam clearly identifies as a Reform Jew. Like others, this seems the foremost source of his Jewish identity. I think this is exclusivity, not of specialness or elitism, but of parochialism. It is not unique to Reform Jews but, in my experience, more prevalent. It begs the question of Sam's allegiance to the larger community. I do not think he, or others like him, would ever slight the broader community in favor of his own "brand." Nonetheless, I do think it has influence over his decision making.

It is also interesting to note that most of Sam's apparent "transcendent" experiences, those that involve some emotional engagement, involve his children. I think this is likely a common, shared experience among parents with young children, and certainly genuine. It will be interesting to see if that wanes as his children get older and what, if anything, might replace it. It is also interesting to note that Sam answered many, if not most, of my questions about what something felt like with physical descriptions or narrative.

His answers about God and things spiritual seemed forced and at the same time genuine, but not complete. It is interesting to note that his IAT shows all the religions bunched together in a cluster, almost directly in the middle of more positive/more negative. I surmise that, in general, Sam does not see religion as an important facet of life. At the same time, he is able to separate the religious aspect of Judaism from the cultural and historical.

If my comments seem critical of Sam, it is only because he and others like him are the future leaders of synagogues. I have no doubt that he will continue to serve his synagogue and would be surprised if he did not become president at some point in the future. His enthusiasm is genuine. However, it is not infectious.

Sam is a synagogue insider and uses what I will term "insider language." Most enthusiastic members share this insider language. However, for those not in-the-know, this language is foreign and off-putting. One of my primary goals is to elicit a common language to express insider truths of experience (their thin slices) in general, common language available to outsiders. I will return to this very important topic in the conclusions. The nascent, theological language of synagogues is an intentional insiders language.

Your Implicit Preference Scale

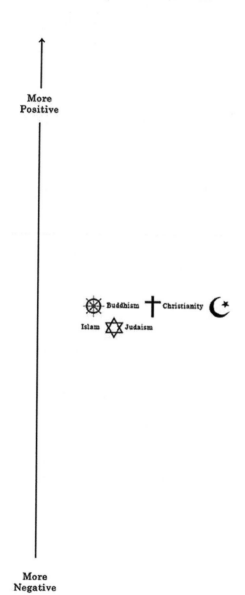

More
Positive

More
Negative

Sheila

Sheila identifies as "just Jewish," though she has a long familial history with a Conservative synagogue and considers herself an active member. She is in the 26 to 39 age group, married, and has two young children. To the survey question about movement affiliation, Sheila answered, "I don't like labels. I like Conservative traditions when I'm at synagogue, except for length. Besides, I prefer to practice my Judaism at home." Sheila's grandfather immigrated to the United States in the late nineteen-teens and her family has been members of the same synagogue since then.

When I asked Sheila to name a positive experience at synagogue, she immediately recounted the celebration of her grandfather's *Yahrzeit*[59] when Sheila was in elementary school. She shared that besides getting to miss the first period of school for that day, her entire family would gather for the morning *minyan* (prayer service). "It was alive then... we would just funnel into the chapel for the *minyan* in the morning. And, then we'd all go back into the kitchen. Everything was sort of relaxed at the synagogue. It wasn't like such an institution as it is today. It was just sort of like everyone's synagogue. We'd go in there and my uncle would start cooking breakfast. He knew where everything was... it's not like he had a position or anything." I asked if she still recognizes her grandfather's *Yahrzeit* and whether it has the same impact. She replied, "I still go, but now it's my dad and I. My brother doesn't really go. My uncle lives in (another city). All those other guys are dead. My cousin doesn't go, just my dad and I. And, to be honest, I'm the one who has to tell my dad, 'hey, you know, pick you up tomorrow at 7:15'."

I asked Sheila to recount a moment in synagogue when she felt alive, fulfilled, or enthused. She quickly replied, "I go back to the *minyan*... I love a *minyan*... there's something special about a lay led service. It lacks pretention... And, there's nothing better. I go, I take all my friends who have lost parents and I take them to the *minyan*, not for them, well slightly for them, but also because I really like it. And just, you can see how cathartic it is for them. (They seem so) proud of doing this *mitzvah*. If you could see the way that makes them feel, and they went a whole year not knowing, not even acknowledging a single emotion about the loss of a parent. And then, something happens during that. Maybe they're crying, maybe they're not. Maybe they're just relieved, maybe it's just a matter of

---

[59] Literally "time of year" in Yiddish referring to the acknowledgment of the date of death of a loved one.

69

like, they didn't realize how stressed they were and it just falls off because (the prayer leader) said something nice. Because they said a prayer for their lost parent. Every time I do that, it's great, I love it."

I asked Sheila to describe the difference between lay led *minyans* and clergy led services. She began by describing the latter as pretentious but then caught herself and described it as formal. She made an interesting comment when she said, "I want to belong to a very Conservative synagogue and not go to it." When pressed, Sheila identified what she sees as incongruities between traditional services and what is actually done in her synagogue's service. She also berated the apparent lack of knowledge she sees in most of her fellow congregants. "How important it is to show up Friday night or Saturday morning, or this that or the other, and 99% of the congregants probably could not even come up with a single verse from any text, probably don't know the difference between Joseph or Joshua, or couldn't come up with the 7 of the 12 tribes, probably don't know who Ephraim is. You know, big characters in our history. I think that's ridiculous."

I responded, "So, would it be a stretch to say that you connect with the learning part of Judaism as well as the communal part?" To this, Sheila shared that she is a *Litvak*[60]. This discovery seemed to be very important to her. "Because the *Litvak* heritage is concentration on study, and maybe in some way my great grandfather concentrated on study, study, study, study, so now it's sort of what appeals to me. It's sort of what I associate is learning, and absorbing, and I guess the price is… there's maybe less spirituality. At least that's hard (spirituality) for me. You know, I don't really care whether or not there's an afterlife or even whether there's a God necessarily, in the context of how we see God. I certainly don't care whether the Torah was divine or man-made or both, or whether the oral law was given entirely to Moses. To me, none of that means anything. What I do know is that, as a code of how to live a life of meaning, and with an ethic and a moral compass, it seemed to work pretty well for a few thousand years… I have a certain numbers of hours I can or am willing to devote to Judaism or Jewish study or whatever. And, I can do that Saturday morning for 2 hours in the synagogue or… I get this out (pulls out a book); I can read this."

Sheila went on to describe her discovery that Jewish text (and accompanying ethical and moral teachings) speak to the issues she actually wrestles with in her daily life. She shared a story of not having the money one week to pay their housekeeper and she was ready to tell her she would pay her the

---

[60]   Referring to Jews of Lithuanian descent during the 19th century. Litvak's had a reputation of placing high value on Jewish learning as part of lifestyle regardless of ethnic affinity.

following week for two weeks (as she had done in the past). During her Jewish reading that week, she discovered that delaying payment to a worker is forbidden in Jewish ethical teachings. "Here I thought I was living this wonderful, ethical life and I knew right and wrong, and I knew I was doing the right things and all that. But, you know, it's maybe because I don't kill anybody and I'm not an adulterer, and I don't steal, maybe now it's not so easy. It's incremental... So, I decided I was sort of looking for some connection. I've always liked the cultural connection. Like, I love going to Israel, and I love Jewish stuff. I mean there is a lot of Jewish stuff in this house. But, this (study) is really fun for me."

I asked Sheila if she felt her connection to Judaism and her community was based on a sense of exploration and learning. She shared an analogy. "You have a globe of water. (The globe has) two different colors of water. There's blue and, say, white, and the blue would be Judaism, and it's 75% or more of this globe. And, so, you know, it's just so much. I don't wanna say take it for granted, but it's just a fact. Like, you know, I don't spend a lot of time trying to figure out or even thinking about where my Judaism is or how I'm Jewish. It's almost like I have ten fingers. Now, why do I have ten fingers? I never give a thought about how many fingers I have or why I'm Jewish. I can tell you where I get the enjoyment out of it. I love talking about Jewish things to my daughter who goes to the (local Jewish school). So, she comes home decently educated for a four-year-old about Jewish stuff, singing songs about Esther. I mean, I don't even need to look at a Jewish calendar. She comes home singing a song and I know what holiday's coming up. That's fun. I really get a kick out of that... We've been bred over generations, and generations, and generations to be studious, think a certain way... And, I really like that; I'm a product of that. I don't mean to say we're better than anybody else. It's just that in our culture, the highest and best trait you can have is to be intelligent, and have a strong knowledge of Torah and Talmud."

Shifting gears, I asked Sheila if she could name a time when she felt a deep sense of belonging to her congregation. She shared that when she was growing up, "I could go anywhere (in the synagogue) I wanted to, and I just felt that completely a part of me, like it's my synagogue. And, I still feel like it's my synagogue. The folks that work there are more temporary than I am." I asked if she still felt that sense of belonging and ownership. Sheila replied, "I do, except that the difference is that the way that Judaism is practiced there is less appealing to me than it was growing up." When I asked her in what way is it different, she shared that firstly she just does not like going to synagogue. The times of the services are not conducive to life with young children. "It just doesn't feel good. It doesn't. It's not restful. So, part of that's the kids. It's hard to get there, you know? Saturday morning is just a big block of time." Alternatively, Sheila shared, "We have Friday night here, and it's wonderful. It's like Shabbat descends on this house."

I pressed Sheila to find out why she is still a member and supports a synagogue, and if that made her feel part of something bigger than herself. She replied, "I certainly don't feel that the synagogue is something bigger than myself. I would say the Federation and the Jewish agencies, you know, ADL (Anti-Defamation League), these are big things. They're bigger than myself. But, the synagogue is like a spoke. It's something that's sort of an interaction. I don't really feel like it's bigger than myself… it's just one more cultural thing that my kids could remember."

It was apparent to me that I was touching a tender nerve and changed subjects. I moved to asking Sheila about spirituality. She shared that her husband loves synagogue and finds great meaning and spiritual connection in synagogue services and Jewish symbolism. He is not Jewish. Sheila said, "I'm very practical, dry."

I asked if she considered studying Talmud and learning to do spiritual exercises or have a spiritual component. "There's a spiritual aspect to it. It's not binary, I don't think. But, if you look at certain texts, you know how much practicality (is) there. The Talmud is extremely practical, even in the way it's divided. It's not even linear, it's subject oriented. To me, that's a very practical way of thinking about things… I think he (referring to her husband) strongly believes in God. He thinks about afterlife. He thinks about all these things that I don't really care about. It is or it isn't. You know what I mean? What comes next, it is or it isn't. So, me believing one thing or another doesn't change a damn thing. So, why am I spending any time on it? That's how I think about it." I asked if there was anything about her childhood she would consider spiritual. "No, nothing comes to mind." I asked if her parents or grandparents ever talked about God. "No."

I asked Sheila if there was a time as an adult when she made the decision that the synagogue was her congregation. "Nope. It was. I was born there. Born into it. So, there was no decision point. The only decision point that could exist would be that it isn't." I asked, "So, almost like an inheritance?" She replied, "Yeah. The same way I know I'm a Jew. And, the only decision point would be not being a Jew, 'cause the de facto, or status quo, or whatever, is, is Jew. It's this synagogue." I asked if she ever thought about looking at someplace else. "Yeah,

I'm constantly thinking about where the right place is for me. I like (another synagogue in town). It's close. I know people there. It's much more informal."

Sheila then shared her dislike of the clergy at her synagogue. I asked, "So, there's something there that says to you, 'even though there are things about this synagogue that don't work for me, and here's a synagogue that might work better, I'm gonna stay where I am'." Sheila replied, "Yeah, right, now we made the decision to stay because I like also seeing my family on High Holiday services. So, what we could do is belong to one and buy seats at another for high holidays. But, we don't go that often so it's not that big a deal."

When I asked about the Reform congregation, Sheila was definitive, "I don't belong there, never will." Referring to this congregation's rabbi, "he's a real congregational rabbi." Then referring to his own congregation's clergy, "If I want a clergyman from our community to speak to an imam or a priest, or write an op-ed, or even give a eulogy at a family member's (funeral), nobody does that better than (my congregation's rabbi). They nail it. (They) probably have 100 IQ points on all of the other rabbis combined. And, that gives you two attributes, an amazing ability to interact intellectually with the larger community and a strong inability to engage personally. And, that's just the way it is. It's usually, I mean, it's hard to find both of those."

I switched to the topic of her survey answers. To the question about whether or not synagogue membership is important, Sheila answered "absolutely." To the question as to whether or not synagogue membership is essential to her Jewish-ness, she replied that it was not. I asked if she sees a contradiction in these two answers. "No. It's important because I'm obligated, I believe, to support Jewish institutions, and I've concluded that Jewish life would suffer greatly without a vibrant synagogue life. So, I think the Jewish culture, the Jewish people, the community, needs a strong synagogue life to thrive. But, when you ask 'do I need a strong synagogue life to have a deep, rich Jewish life in my family, in my house'... I don't believe that's essential."

On the survey, she answered that she had been involved in synagogue leadership and that it was a negative experience. Sheila clarified that she had been on the congregation's board. She said, "I've been on a lot of boards. There's two types, and I'm just gonna generalize. There are boards that do things. And, there are boards that (are) sort of an advisory board to staff that do everything. I mean, I'm not gonna pine on governments here, but I know where I feel like I belong, you know, where it's a good use of my time, and it's in the former... I was assured (when) I went on the long-range planning committee, I said, 'well, here's my concern, is that from what I understand, the board just shows up once a month, and then listens, and then votes yay and that's it'. And, she (one recruiting Sheila for board position) says 'well, that's not true'. And, I said 'well that's exciting, I'm glad to hear that you believe that, and I'll do it'. So, I did that for a year and it was a tough year, because it turns out that that's not what anybody wants... So, I felt that that was negative because I came up with all these great ideas in the committee... and they were shot down as just not relevant and not needed... Every hour I spend outside of the house, I want it to be as valuable and meaningful as possible."

I asked Sheila how she would describe Judaism to someone who knew nothing about religion. "It can be a smorgasbord. And, for me, it's a way to figure out how to live your life, and how to be connected through 5,000 years of history. How to be connected from generation to generation to generation to generation. And, it's a sense of belonging and identity... As long as we have organized religion, which I'm not sure it was a good thing for humankind, but since we have it, I'm happy to be a Jew."

Me: So, can I surmise that your connection to the previous generations is really fulfillment of a connection to future generations?

Sheila: Yeah, and also because those generations are responsible for all those things, they're the ones who have given so much time and energy and thought into how we should live a moral life, and ethical life, and what's important. Where to find meaning in life and there's some examples of ... finding meaning in the smallest things. Even big changes, we survived. And then, here we are now (and) we always have our challenges. It's not like our generation is the first time. I imagine they were all lamenting the death of Judaism. And, now we have our own (issues), in our own generation to worry about - intermarriage and assimilation and all those things, and so, you know, they all did their part to preserve a very noble way of life. So, I feel like I want to do that too, like it's sort of one of my obligations, to figure out what I can do to make sure that Judaism continues, and I don't know what form or another, I'm not the kind of caliber to make those decisions. But, you know, my family unit, I can just do what I can do."

I confess that while I found Sheila sometimes elusive and unwilling to look deeply into some issues, I thoroughly enjoyed this interview. I found her ability to be candid about her beliefs even in the face of apparent (to me at least) incongruence and inconsistency, refreshing and eye-opening. Sheila was able to see her connection to her congregation realistically, and even though some aspects are obviously problematic, they are not so problematic that they become defining of the relationship.

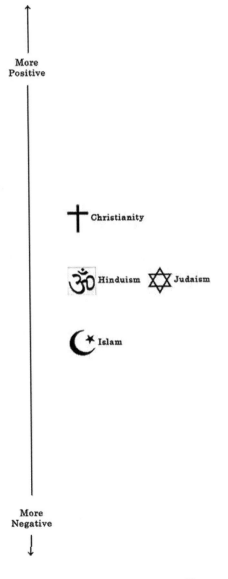

Your Implicit Preference Scale

More
Positive

✝ Christianity

🕉 Hinduism ✡ Judaism

☪ Islam

More
Negative

At times, I found Sheila's answers to hint at a deep seated ethnic romanticism, using Hoffman's definition of ethnicity as doing what comes naturally, but with no transcendent purpose. In Sheila's case, I found myself rethinking the term "transcendent purpose." Like other interviewees, Sheila's dialogue eschews spirituality and its connotations of connection to something greater in the universe. However, her actions, including her adult-found interest in textual study say the opposite. Hoffman himself writes, "It is difficult to comprehend the extent to which Judaism casts study as a spiritual enterprise because, in the modern world, the act of study has become so thoroughly secularized."[61] So, while Sheila does not see her actions as spiritual, Judaism would certainly permit them to be seen as such. Therefore, one may surmise there is transcendent purpose and the definition of ethnicity does not apply.

What, then, are Sheila's connections? Again, using Hoffman as defining authority, I see Sheila's actions as a cultural connection to Judaism, or "the totality of wisdom, practices, folkways and so forth that constitute what we choose to remember of Jewish experience."

Sheila's interview opened up for me a new perspective on congregational affinity and allegiance. While before I considered answers like hers to be petty and without thought, there is a great deal of cultural and historical information that defines and informs her decisions. That she is unaware of them seems immaterial other than enabling others to transmit these "selling points" to others. However, like Sam, Sheila uses insider's language, accessible only to other insiders. That I had to read the transcript of her interview to realize the full value in her meaning gives further indication of the vague and imprecise nature of insider language.

---

[61] Rabbi Lawrence Hoffman, *The Journey Home: Discovering the Deep Spiritual Wisdom of the Jewish Tradition* (Boston: Beacon Press, 2002), 69.

Vince

Vince is in the 40 to 65 age group and a member of a Reform congregation. He is the third generation of his family to be members of this same congregation. He considers himself a lifelong Reform Jew, and is a regular worship attendee and very active in other synagogue affairs.

When I asked Vince about a positive experience in his synagogue, his answer was his wedding. I asked what was positive about it. He replied, "The rabbi who was not always known for being that open to interfaith marriages, was willing to marry us before (his wife) converted. And, you know, it's just wonderful to have friends and family around to celebrate something important in a place that was comfortable for me in a spiritual (way)." I asked if there were other things that made it positive. He answered (and I was confused by his answer), "It wouldn't have been. Had I been married by someone who is appointed for the day to do it, a judge, or at any other place that didn't feel like my home, or not under a *chuppah* (wedding canopy)... If it didn't have the elements of a Jewish wedding, if it didn't have my traditions in it, it wouldn't have felt the same way. So, it was that, it was the comfort, like a comfortable pair of jeans, or what you know. It's what you know, and where you know it. That was why."

I pressed him to identify what was comfortable about the traditions at his wedding. Rather than naming individual traditions, he again related the familiarity of the setting... "Being walked down the aisle by my parents, the *chuppah*, seeing the rabbi and the cantor under the *chuppah*, knowing who they are, my sisters and that kind of thing." Pressing farther, I asked what comfortable looked like in that setting. He answered, "... just knowing the traditions, knowing the rituals, knowing what's going to happen next and why. Understanding the context of it, that's all comfortable. And, I know that comfort level would have been diminished being in another synagogue in another city, or another synagogue in this city, or whatever. Or, anywhere but a synagogue."

Sensing there was something else present for Vince, I asked if he could imagine the same rabbi, same cantor, same *chuppah*, and same setting, but this time in a hotel. Would it have been different? He immediately replied, "Yes... I was consecrated there and I was confirmed there, and our family had celebrated all its happy occasions there. There was something that adds an element of comfort and warmth and meaning to me." He shared that his family has a "... substantial history with the congregation."

I asked Vince if he could name a time when he felt enlivened or enthused by something at his synagogue. He shared that his first thought was sounding the *shofar* (ritual ram's horn blown on the High Holy Days). "I used to do it for the kids, but when I became the *baal tokea* (literally "master of the blast") for the first time, for the whole congregation, services of 1,500 people or whatever we have in there during those services. It's pretty amazing. I got applause, just kind of weird in the middle of a religious service, and the rabbi did the touchdown sign, you know? The rabbi was sort of blown away too. Not that I play it well, it just sounded different than other people do. And, (insofar) that it was different and it had a whole different feeling than we'd ever known... Just warm, beautiful, so it was kind of an amazing moment. (I) felt very connected at that moment."

I asked to what he felt connected. "Well, to the institution, but also really to Judaism, to my ancestors that went before, and to people in the congregation. And I, you know, in the years that followed, I've done it now for 30 years. I mean, just like I was this really old dude. You know, I'm only 55 and I've done it for 30 years. But, in the first maybe 5 to 10 years, people in the congregation would come up, and it was very meaningful for them, and they would thank me for doing that ... And, it makes me emotional to talk about it. And, that was also intensely meaningful that people were touched. That's another piece of (my congregation's history) that's so important... This notion of members [men and women] having equality in service and in service to the congregation, and religious rights and things was powerful."

I asked if Vince could identify a moment or time of a sense of belonging. He said the same experience of blowing the shofar that first time and each subsequent time over the years. Then he shared, "... but the difference between membership and belonging is certainly clearer to me. So, belonging, for me, the first step is that you want to be there. But, beyond that, that you also feel like you're welcomed there. That you know people there that you can say hello, even though I know more faces than names... Part of that being part (of) this bigger thing, that we're people (who) are familiar and comfortable, and I feel like I'm wanted. I feel like I have friends, I have family there."

I asked, "Is that sense of belonging part of something bigger than yourself?" Vince replied, "Yeah, sure it is, for me it is, I know it's also not universally felt at (my synagogue) in particular... it's not a warm place. It still isn't. We're trying, we're working at it, but it's hard to fight the culture you've had for generations. But, yes, it is something big. I mean, it's being part of the secret handshake, if you will. And, I don't mean that in a privileged sense. I mean just knowing, being around people who know the same. It's the same sort of something bigger that I felt when I went down to the first and third nights of *Hannukah* on a (cruise) ship. There are 500 chairs in the room. And, it was just this sort of tingly feeling that we all know the secret handshake. We all will say the prayers. It will be the same words. It doesn't matter that they're from Mexico City and these people are from New York City, and those people are from wherever. We all know the same words. So, that was that feeling of part of something bigger."

I asked Vince to describe this feeling, this tingly feeling of connectedness. He answered, "… complete and utter belonging. You know, when people make the jokes, you get them immediately… it's because you all know that same joke and you can make a joke with each other. You know you know." Pressing for more clarity, I asked if this connection is deeper with another Jew than with a non-Jew and, if so, if he knew why. "I think it's all these common denominators. I appreciate anybody's path to their meaning. I mean, whatever they find, as long as you do no harm to other people. However, if someone finds meaning and fulfillment or whoever they view as their higher power, live and let live. I'm happy for them. Being with people who believe in one God, or who at least the preponderance who do, I am sure there are plenty of people questioning that. We don't know what that means. That's good for me. I like the idea that I can interpret God in my own way. Nobody's (in Judaism) telling me that I was born with sin and what's important is right now. Not when I die. So, all those things are a deeper level where you can connect with people that feel the same things, by and large. We are Jewish. We're going to disagree."

I asked Vince what comes to mind when I say the word "spirituality". He replied, "the kinda spirituality that doesn't really mean anything to me at all and it, and it seems kinda weird. You know, kinda pagan-ey kind of stuff. But, for me or my own religious belief, what comes to mind is actually being on the enlightenment path and reading from the prayer book all together, because we all say the same words and we're actually feeling beyond the words, feeling something into the words and, and around an experience that's deeper meaning than just the experience itself, or the reading itself, or the worship itself, or whatever. It certainly goes beyond that, into heart and soul."

I asked Vince if he gets this sense of spirituality in synagogue. "Sometimes I get it with the singing." At a recent event, he attended a session on "…guided meditation, and not sort of dolphins swimming through the waters kind of guided meditation, but close your eyes and really meditate, and with some guiding, and it was (an) amazing experience… I came out of there like Jell-O. It was great. It was refreshing, but not in a sort of physically invigorating way, but in sort of an emotionally invigorating, and spiritually invigorating way. There's different ways to get there." I asked if there were things he would consider spiritual. "The life cycle moments of my life; my marriage, my children's births, sadly my mom's death."

I asked if he thought there was spirituality in his childhood. "No, my parents were Jews because their parents were Jews and they were Classical Reform and, you know, my dad will talk about the Classic Reform service and say this (current services) is 'that banjo service'. It was high church and the Union Prayer Book said 'leader' and not 'rabbi,' right? And, it was about doing good in the world. It was about caring about the right issues, and the biggest issue for me when I was a kid was civil rights. I wrote letters to President Johnson and I wrote letters to Mrs. Martin Luther King expressing my condolences, and that kind of stuff. So, that was big, that was huge, but there was no teaching (that) that is what Judaism is about. For my parents, I'm sure it wasn't about that from their parents. It was not about obligation, but duty, responsibility. And then, to be in the world. Their friend, Mrs. Levinson, said to me one time, it's the quote from Micah, 'Do justice, love mercy, and walk humbly with your God'. In her words, she quoted that and said the rest is all bullshit. So, that's pretty much how my childhood was. This was about me finding out for myself, which is okay."

I asked if he knew to whom or what they felt responsible. "It was to Judaism, but it was to their next generation, the kids. It was to each other, and it was about the world. Making the world a better place. I certainly got that growing up. Probably the highest duty of a Jew (was) to go out and walk with Martin Luther King or to serve on the civil rights commission. That was what we were about. Yeah, you went to services, but not all the time. We did do Shabbat, but it was this little pamphlet that had been scotch-taped together so many times that it was yellow, and I can recite it to you right now, because it became totally subconscious... But, it wasn't spiritual, it was just rote sort of thing."

I then asked if looking back he thought that those things his parents taught – duty, responsibility, improving the world, etc. maybe had a spirituality to them. "Yeah, probably so. I don't think they would have thought of it that way, but I see it that way. I think I'm in that generation that still believes in the responsibility, duty, and handing it down to your children. I don't think the generation that's getting it handed to them cares, and they're going to move. So, they don't feel that same connection to an institution. I mean, I think they will when they come back to visit and all that stuff. You know, you sort of never forget your first synagogue.

Your home synagogue if you will. Like, you know, your first kiss, your first love, or whatever. It's all part of your psychology history. But, I'm sorta in between. I think those things... those were impressed upon me, and I got it."

I asked Vince if he could name the moment as an adult when he decided the synagogue was his spiritual home. His answer, "That's an interesting one. 'Cause I never thought it wasn't, you know ... maybe I, as an adult, (got the) understanding of that when I got married."

When I asked Vince if there were attributes of the synagogue he did not like, he spent quite a lot of time naming problem areas. "I've always felt very accepted, and have belonged to it. But, I don't like that people find it to be cold, and that it probably is. You know, I don't feel that and never have." ...We made decisions on the cheap... that it's worthy of your time, energy and dollars. So, we've always acted cheap." ...and then, finally, we're slow to change. We're just so stuck in our ways, you know. And, that's particularly irksome to me right now, because I've had a good relationship with the clergy. Not everyone has. I have had one over the years. A very good relationship. But, the music, the performance style is really bugging me now."

I asked what would be worthy of member's dollars. "Well, you know what, it's an interesting thing, and again, this is about how I see today. And, maybe I see 40, 50 years ago or maybe even just 30 (years) ago, we're a completely rabbi led culture. So, when (former rabbi) left and everybody said 'whew, you know, we need the anti-(former rabbi) and we got the anti-(former rabbi)', the inmates had no idea how to run the asylum, and so it's been chaos for 15 years. And frankly, deficient rabbi leadership, because that's what we said we wanted. Then we were afraid to do an interim and we picked the guy that wasn't top of the list and we got what we did. So, I think that what's worthy of their dollars – is the kind of leadership that makes you feel and want to come to temple, want to be part of something bigger. Cuz, you know, what's the point of organized religion if you haven't gotten along? I mean, I can put a little shrine up here and be done with it, you know? But, that makes you wanna come near, makes you wanna volunteer, makes you want to give your dollars, and I think it's very interesting. I do think that there was a pretty healthy... we still acted cheap, we always have, but there's a healthy financial commitment during the times when the rabbis were pretty spectacular rabbis. This commitment to a strong spiritual leader, whatever that looks like for people, makes the difference. That is what brings people in, or moves people, or makes them feel part of something, or helps them understand their Judaism better, you know, teaches, whatever extra characteristic it is, and I think we have it again. I think we got the mojo back."

81

I asked what he thought that leadership mojo is and once it is back, what does the congregation get. "You come for some other reason. And, you learn something. You know you're taught because that's what rabbi means. You know, you actually get taught something. You hear something that challenges you or makes you look deeper into something. Or think deep, more deeply about something. For the first time, Shabbat means something to you. Oh, this is what it (means), this is why it is so phenomenal or profound. That your family feels taken care of. You know, that the person steps up, or they call and they ask how you're doing. And, those kinds of things. I think personal connection-relationship is vitally important. And, if you're a person (referring to rabbi) who's uncomfortable with that, especially at times when we need that the most, you're going to turn people (away). No one wants to go to an institution that has no interest in that. But, when you have someone who can express that interest it means everything."

In the survey, Vince answered that synagogue membership is essential to his Jewishness. I asked him what is essential about being a synagogue member. "Well, it's kinda like eating a meal alone; the food is just not that good and you can't share with everybody, you can't poach on their plate, you know? Or, going to a movie alone, cuz you have no one to talk to about the movie afterwards. I mean, it's really truly about sharing that experience. Even if you walk in and you just say hello to people, and then you walk out. What's essential is being in the same place that you all came to on your own volition. You learn or are moved by something during that time together. I have plenty of prayer on my own and all that, but it's just not enough. I need to be in a place where other people are praying too."

I asked how this is different from being together with a group of Jews at a Jewish Community Center (JCC) or Federation event. "Well, you're there because you care about Judaism… Certainly, their goals are laudable to support the Jewish community here and all over the world. But, it just seems to be about the campaign. Some programming. But, it's all sort of programming to get you to the campaign… What's unique about being in a group of Jews in the synagogue and being with the group of Jews somewhere else? I don't know. It's like being at home with those people. You're at a place that's your home. All of your home. And, maybe people… if I were in a group of Jews at synagogue, some of which didn't grow up here or don't feel so fondly, they wouldn't answer this question the same way. But, for me, it's being at my home with the people that I shared things with. I share thoughts and beliefs and practices and ritual with (them). And, it's about that. I mean, there's an element of it that's about commune. Clearly, there's an element that's about community. I'm with my own community. I'm with my people. So, some of it's about social community. But, it's also about spiritual community. That we're all there for some purpose, whatever our individual purposes are, but we come together. And, we say the same prayers in the same order, in different ways. And, we get different things out of them. But, we're still in the community doing that. That's what changes it for me."

Pressing the issue, I asked if he could imagine a group meeting in the synagogue and then the same group meeting at his home; could he articulate a difference. "There's no ark. There are no things that mean (something). I have lots of Judaica in my home. But, it's not the same as having an ark with a Torah."

On the survey, Vince identified that he had held several leadership positions in his congregation. He identified being on the board and chairing several committees. On the survey, he also noted that these experiences were neutral. I asked him what was neutral about his experiences. "I had been on the board before and went off. It was quite miserable for the first tenure, and that was because, again, this notion of we are fighting our culture trying to move to another place. It was about reviewing the rabbi. Board governance is necessary, but it didn't having any meaningful component to it. I joined it in the first place when I was asked because it was after (former rabbi) was non-renewed. I think he was gone and I thought, you know, quit bitching. Just get in there. You have an obligation to get in and do something if you really feel that way. Improve the place. So, that's when I joined. Okay, so that's 6 years of my tenure with our immediate past rabbi. And, it started off with a friendly relationship, and then I saw he was a person uniquely unqualified to be a rabbi. So, I would go to temple and I'd have the dialogue under my head, instead of praying I'd be going, 'why is he talking about his family again? Why is he talking about xyz? Why does every sentence begin with I? I, I, I.' And, I quit going. I mean, that's why, because I just didn't find meaning and we didn't seem to be making progress. So, that said, if you ask me that question again today, I would say I don't know what the responses are in the multiple choice, but I would say, I'm hopeful about the ability to make change."

I asked how his attitude and energy have changed regarding board leadership. "I feel differently about it. I will say this rabbi puts it in a... it's not that he just does a *d'var* (akin to sermon), or we all say prayer or whatever. But, he actually puts service in a spiritual context. It gives you a reason why you're there. Why it's important for you to be there. Why it's important to Judaism that you're serving. And somehow, I feel like we have an opportunity to make change. And, I want to be there to help do that. I wanna help drive it actually. It's what I want to do."

83

I asked Vince about his family. He is the fourth generation of members at this synagogue. He describes his great-grandparents as "pretty close" to original founders. He shared on the survey that he was not very active in Jewish activities outside synagogue until adulthood. I asked what changed for him. "So, what changed was probably the either *shofar* sounding or parenthood. Probably more parenthood than anything else, cuz even after we got married we didn't go very often. Parenthood really draws you in. Which is the hope we have for the 20's and 30's, right? How can an independent *minyan* take care of religious school and all that? They can't. So, you just hope that that means at that point people (or you) figure out how to do that before, so that they're there and ready to go or something."

When I asked Vince if he had anything else to share, unlike most interviewees he did. "I can tell you I'm in a different place as regards... I mean, I've been committed to the institution forever. You know, if you're looking for someone ambivalent, I'm not that person. And, I will remain that person. And, I will remain that, I'm sure, throughout my life, unless something really drastic happens. I have to say, too, that this notion of community and relationship just became so underscored by my mom's illness and her death."

These final comments also underscore my experience with Vince. He is a committed member of his congregation and sees it as integral to his life. In him, I found someone who is willing to explore the issues of 'why' without the hesitation and discomfort of some interviewees. I think this is in part because he is not uncomfortable with looking at spirituality and spiritual language. While he still noted discomfort with 'Christian language' like "ministry", he also recognized there are parallels in Judaism and their direct effect on synagogue participation.

However, Vince is perhaps the greatest example of a synagogue insider. He identifies Judaism with a "secret handshake." He admits that his synagogue is neither warm nor friendly, but through his participation (blowing the shofar as an example), he knows the secret handshake. I do not think he would easily admit that Judaism is akin to an exclusive, private club, but his language reveals otherwise.

I found Vince insightful about synagogue leadership, though sometimes a bit simplistic. This is in part because he has made a very intentional and deliberate attempt at being educated Jewishly, and about synagogues and congregational development.

I think it is no coincidence that, at least for Vince, there seems to be a direct correlation between knowledge of what is possible and how to affect change and positive feelings towards his congregation. Additionally, Vince's IAT (Figure 8) results show very high positive feeling towards Judaism. Again, I think it is no coincidence that he has high regard for Judaism and this seems correlated to his positive attitude about his synagogue.

Your Implicit Preference Scale

CONCLUSIONS

One goal of this project was to create a narrative for synagogues to express compelling, rational promotion of synagogue membership to those who are suspicious of the organized Jewish community. Essentially, tools to help synagogues better market their offerings. My hope was that stalwart, committed synagogue members had some deeply entrenched, unconscious knowledge of the value of membership somewhere in their collective psyches. Using Cognitive Task Analysis (CTA), I hoped to unseat this knowledge. I believe success, or lack thereof, is subjective.

On the one hand, there certainly is some gold uncovered during the interviews. One stated goal was uncovering patterns of Jewish experience that reflect the importance of the synagogue, and there were some. They include:

1. **Size does matter.** Almost every one of the interviewees mentioned congregation size at some time. For some, like Arnie and Aviva, size was a determining if not primary factor in congregation choice. Others, like Michelle, commented that her congregation was too big, and while this was not a choice determinant, it affected comfort, satisfaction levels, and participation.

2. **Community.** Every one of the interviewees talked about synagogue as community, both distinct from and part of the larger Jewish community. For some, this tied in with congregation size; that smaller congregations have a better sense of community. For those who remained in large synagogues, several actively sought their own communities within the congregation. Michelle summed up the sense of community by equating the feeling of community with "knowing there is a place for me."

3. **Synagogues need to reflect real life; be responsive.** No one was clearer about this than Sheila who lamented that worship attendance just did not work for her young family. Her comment was that "synagogue life doesn't fit with real life." Michelle made the same sorts of comments referring back

to years ago when her now grown children were young. She related that going to Friday night services with her husband and young children was a wonderful family experience, "...probably the singing and the feeling of community, belonging to a community, that made it feel positive. And, I guess I walked out of there feeling good about being there and then heading to dinner, as a family." She quickly shared that they stopped regularly attending with their children because it was not convenient and conducive to children. Sheila was very clear that it is those moments when her text study leads to the discovery of "direct parallels between Judaism and real life" that Judaism comes to life for her.

4. **Meaning**[62]. Though spirituality is difficult for many of the interviewees to articulate and, in some cases, come to terms with, it seems clear that Jews are looking for meaning in their lives. Arnie, who was quite at ease with the conversation of spirituality, talked about "communal experiences as spiritual experiences." Others, including Marcie, who was least articulate about spirituality, spoke of a sense of belonging and connectedness. Sheila, who was perhaps the most cerebral in her approach to Judaism, preferring study over practice, conceded there is a greater purpose to study and that, "there's a spiritual aspect to it." Arnie was able to articulate the connection between meaning and community when he said, "spirituality is a sense of belonging to something greater than oneself and a sense of connectedness."

5. **A sense of home.** I distinguish this sense of "home" from community because the word came up so often. Almost all the interviewees said something about "home" in their interviews, intimating that they sought a sense of connection more personal and intimate than that of community. Aviva spoke of the "feeling of being home... warmth and the welcoming feeling, comfort, relationships." It seems no coincidence that those who spoke strongly of smaller congregational size also used the home metaphor most often.

My second stated goal was to provide a narrative to those suspicious of the traditional Jewish community. Since this is a qualitative research project, this determination is, again, subjective. Repeating the statement I made in the introduction, qualitative research is distinguished from other forms of research by

---

[62] I will admit that I am making assumptions about the word "meaning" and that it is related to spirituality. None of the interviewees used the word "meaning" without my using it first.

the idea that "the word is not simply 'out there' waiting to be discovered" but occurs in the ways in which we choose to view it.[63]

Since qualitative research is subjective, I will offer an assessment of my performance in providing that narrative for those suspicious folk – I failed, at least partially. I had a preconceived notion of what this narrative language would look like, something akin to Christian theological language. Instead, what I discovered was the insider language highlighted in Sam and Vince's interviews. Instead of an inclusive language, this is an exclusive language. Rather than discovering a language to share Judaism and synagogue value with those outside the established community, I discovered that those inside the community are using language that excludes others.

Synagogues are ethnic-centered, exclusive institutions. I stated this and the evidence to support it in the beginning chapter. They must become inclusive and intentional organizations with a conscious, evolving story going on. As Rabbi Lawrence Hoffman wrote to me in an email exchange, synagogues must be intentional about creating "public language that provides a story for synagogues to use regarding potential members and to offset suspicions."[64]

Hoffman's "public language" is his interpretation of the work of Juergen Habermas who has worked on the issue of religion and secularity, which he says creates a "public space" for them to coexist. Habermas deals with whether religion has a say in the body politic. According to Hoffman, Habermas says yes, but only if it is able to translate its particularistic language into one that secular conversationalists can understand and debate.[65] In essence, a language that is part of the shared public; shared conversational language accessible to both religious and secular thinkers. As it relates to synagogues, they must find a shared, public, secular language in which both insiders and outsiders can converse. I posit that the language already exists and perhaps it is simply a matter of the insiders using less insider language.

Hoffman goes on to explain something he calls a "language of meaning." "There are three meanings: official, public, and idiosyncratic. People who use insider language use official meanings: they are not amenable to public discourse in the Habermas sense. Public meanings are the area of public discourse – the things we might say about our experience in words other than what ethnic and

---

63 John Swinton and Harriet Mowatt, *Practical Theology and Qualitative Research* (London: SCM Press, 2007), 29.
64 Lawrence Hoffman, email interview, 1 November 2012.
65 Ibid.

insider Judaism give us... Vince [as an example] uses idiosyncratic meaning, 'I still love the place, despite its failures, because I blew the shofar in it for thirty years!' What is an outsider to make of this? It refers to his private experience only."[66]

This public language must be one that everyone already uses. By default, I think it is a secular language. This should not be problematic for synagogues who already embrace secular language in areas like lay leadership, business practices, and financial dealings.

A major obstacle is finding public meanings for some of these insider concepts. Using Vince as an example, what does he mean when he talks about the secret handshake? It was apparent in the interview that he felt like I would understand his meaning because he assumed I was also an insider. The difficulty comes about when pressing him and others to articulate what they mean. They do not know, at least not readily. Herein lays the value of CTA to dig deeper in order to elicit intended meaning.

Michelle spoke of feeling connected to something bigger than her when she was in a space with other Jews, be it at a conference or in Israel. However, she was unable to name the feeling or explain why she felt it. She spoke of being with others who had a "shared history and a shared bond", but was unable to explain either. When I pressed her, it was clear that her inability to explain this bothered her, and I gather (and hope) she will think more deeply about these feelings and why she has them.

On the positive side, several of the interviews established that there is the capacity for people who love synagogues to become intentional enough to have such a narrative and learn to better express it. While I did not spend enough time with the participants to create such a narrative, I believe I have demonstrated the capacity to create it. We must create opportunities to have these public discussions that are as relevant and engaging as other public events like those in the arts, politics, general community welfare gatherings, and even sports. Synagogues must create transcendent language that uses public language to tell their stories. We must find relativistic terms to replace words like mitzvoth[67], perhaps with spirituality; Israel as a concept and not just a place; Torah with something more personal like life guidance; and certainly God as something personal rather than the religious school concept of a force 'out there' to be reckoned with.

---

[66] Ibid.
[67] Literally, "a commandment". It has also become used to mean "a good deed done out of religious duty".

Getting to a narrative that allays fears and suspicions is akin to changing the culture of synagogues; it will happen very slowly and over a long period of time. Unfortunately, it is also akin to the chicken and egg metaphor – what needs to change first, the culture or the conversation? The answer is both. I do believe there are people, my interviewees included, who could speak in positive terms about their own synagogue experiences and in a way that could help alleviate the fears and suspicions of other Jews. However, I am not sure this skill is innate or even readily accessible for the general Jewish community.

The apparent lesson is that professional intervention is necessary to better tease out this narrative, and then train members to talk in positive terms about their experiences. It is not my goal or place to suggest those professionals, only to observe the language and skills necessary for American Jews to talk positively about their synagogues. Its attributes are not inherent or perhaps lost, if ever part of the Jewish communal psyche. However, knowing that there are some projects and consultants who are having some success changing the culture of synagogues leads me to think professional intervention is necessary for systemic change.

That the Jewish philanthropic community is not seeking or creating these initiatives uncovers another obstacle to systemic change. This will not happen quickly or easily. However, the desire is evident, at least in those interviewed for this project, and I would posit that the need is present in the community. Given the current trends away from synagogue affiliation with nothing comprehensive filling that gap, this is a problem lacking solution(s).

Finding a theological language proved the most difficult aspect of the project. I was hopeful that by scrutinizing the inner depths of committed synagogue members' thoughts I would find sharable and exploitable commonalities. I did not. While trends and patterns were easily identifiable, shared language akin to language expressing transcendence was nearly vacant. Only a couple of the respondents had any comfort distinguishing their synagogue experience as distinct from another club or association. While many easily spoke in business terms about the operational aspects of their congregation, few could really offer substance when speaking of their congregational experience. Several were quick to bring God into the conversation about their synagogue, but pushed beyond the clichéd "say what you think the interviewer wants to hear" language, there appeared nothing of substance.

As stated in the introduction, formal, propositional theology is problematic for Judaism. As Borowitz and the other Jewish theologians have written, Jews have responded to modern culture ideologically rather than theologically. As quoted earlier, "When such issues arise in their (contemporary Jewish intellectuals) work, they do not concentrate their intellectual energies on them and seek to give a systematic – that is, a detailed and coherent – account of what they believe and why."[68] My research did little to dissuade this premise. But, not entirely.

That my subjects were nearly universally cautious of spirituality, both literally and figuratively, leads me to believe there is something inherently missing in their Jewish lives. Taken as a whole, this group, predominantly those in the 40 to 65 age range, was very uncomfortable with spirituality. However, most remarked that in some way they wished they were more spiritual, i.e. more comfortable with either the concept or practice.

I think this is an important distinction when taken in the context of research on younger Jews. Repeating my context, ethnic Judaism as Hoffman defines it (as a nostalgic yearning for Jewish folkways) will not sustain modern American Judaism. The community is now in the second and third generation of American Jews who have little or no nostalgic connection to the "Old Country" Yiddishkeit of their parents, grandparents, and great grandparents. Additionally, emigration from countries like Iran, Iraq, Turkey, and North Africa has brought Jews who never had this ethnic identity, theirs being a historic connection to Sephardic[69] Judaism, not Ashkenazic[70].

Judaism is more than a religion – it is also a culture, an ethnicity (or used to be), a set of traditions, and a unique history. I contend that Judaism as a religion needs new emphasis. This, too, is problematic since there is wide divergence in practice, adherence, and level of emphasis in all Jewish communities. American Jews are unique in that they have choices regarding movement affiliation and therefore the divergence in practice and adherence, but this uniqueness is not an insurmountable stumbling block. Many might disagree with my thesis regarding emphasis on Judaism as religion. Even so, it is clear that American Judaism, and by association American synagogues, need new focus.

---

[68] Eugene Borowitz, *Choices in Modern Jewish Thought* (New Jersey: Behrman House, 1995), 17.
[69] A general term referring to the descendants of Spanish-Portuguese Jews who lived in the Iberian Peninsula before their expulsion in the Alhambra Decree in 1492.
[70] Jews descended from the medieval Jewish communities along the Rhine in Germany from Alsace in the south to the Rhineland in the north.

Jews are less spiritual than their Christian neighbors, so says researchers Steven M. Cohen and Lawrence Hoffman[71]. If one compares these interviewees to Cohen and Hoffman's conclusions, they track with the mainstream. Cohen and Hoffman's study revealed that across the board, Jews scored lower than Christians on spirituality. However, even the researchers admit that the scale is inherently corrupted since it is based on a secular/Christian language and scale. As I and others have already noted, Jews react negatively to Christian spiritual language, so the comparison is troubling at best. However, Cohen and Hoffman's research did reveal the same kind of discomfort with things spiritual that my interviewees shared. And again, while many seek something transcendent, their internal, unconscious biases keep them from fully exploring these interests.

Age is a factor. Referring again to Cohen and Hoffman, those respondents in middle age were most uncomfortable with things spiritual. However, younger Jews appear more comfortable with spirituality, "... we find more elevated spirituality among the youngest adults."[72] As Kelman and Schonberg's research showed, Jews are more intimate with their non-Jewish neighbors than ever before.[73] Jews live, work, go to school, and socialize with non-Jews at higher rates than ever in Jewish-American history. Intermarriage is no longer a stigma in the liberal Jewish world and is nearly de rigueur. Intermarriage rates are above 50% and continue climbing. Fascinatingly, as Jews marry non-Jews, their non-Jewish spouse's influence increases the Jewish spouse's spirituality. In other words, non-Jewish comfort with things spiritual is making Jews more comfortable with things spiritual. Interviewee Sheila brought this issue to light in describing how her non-Jewish husband is very comfortable with spiritual language and actually seeks Jewish ways to enhance his spirituality. Conversely, Sheila never thought much about these issues but now recognizes, at least, that she lacks the ability to think and discuss things spiritual.

As a consequence of intermarriage, younger Jews (many of whom are the children of these Jewish/non-Jewish marriages) have much less difficulty talking about and exploring spirituality. As reported by Cohen and Hoffman, "... a child

---

[71] Steven M. Cohen and Lawrence Hoffman, "How Spiritual Are America's Jews? Narrowing the Spirituality Gap Between Jews and Other Americans," S3K Report (March 2009), 12.
[72] Steven M. Cohen and Lawrence Hoffman, "How Spiritual Are America's Jews? Narrowing the Spirituality Gap Between Jews and Other Americans," S3K Report (March 2009), 12.
[73] Ari Kelman and Eliana Schonberg, *Legwork, Framework, Artwork: Engaging the Next Generation of Jews* (Colorado: The Rose Community Foundation, 2008), 10-11.

growing up with at least one non-Jewish parent will more likely resonate with spirituality."[74]

So what? If synagogues are going to remain relevant they must address these issues. The research, including this study, says they are not. Again, Cohen and Hoffman: "Nonetheless, the kind of spirituality that we see celebrated so popularly, the kind of thing we tested here, does have proponents among Jews, especially young Jews; and within the NextGen (or "young Jew") category, among the Orthodox and Extended Jews-By-Choice in particular. Since those are the two growth sectors of the Jewish population, we can affirm our Synagogue 3000 (S3K) encouragement for synagogues to become spiritual communities. Given the limitations to the spirituality language, especially among older Jews who still largely control synagogue policy, that openness to spirituality will not come easily. But, come it must. We feel that is especially the case for non-Orthodox synagogues where Jewish identity is less certain, and Jews-by-choice more numerous."[75] Also in this same research, we asked people: 'Suppose you could find your ideal synagogue. Would you find it essential, desirable, unimportant or not desirable for the rabbi to talk about God, the afterlife, ultimate meaning, and spiritual issues?'

• 76% of our respondents said it was essential or desirable that the rabbi talk about God.

• 52% said it was essential or desirable for rabbis to talk about the afterlife.

• 73% said it was essential or desirable for rabbis to talk about ultimate meaning.

• 78% said it was essential or desirable for rabbis to talk about spiritual issues."[76]

Nothing is definitive, but this is compelling data, especially since it includes all respondents to their survey – young, middle aged, and seniors.

And finally, as reported by Cohen and Hoffman, "… we return to the issue of language. To the extent that we lack a native Jewish language to describe spirituality, we are hampered by having to discuss it in language borrowed from Christianity. We believe some of the low scores that we found may be a response

---

[74] Steven M. Cohen and Lawrence Hoffman, "How Spiritual Are America's Jews? Narrowing the Spirituality Gap Between Jews and Other Americans," S3K Report (March 2009), 11.
[75] Ibid, 14.
[76] Ibid, 14.

to the language as much as to the experience, since without language to describe it, experience (if it exists at all) is fleeting – it cannot even be put into words and shared. As familiarity with the language grows, we expect spirituality to grow as well."[77]

Again, we are back to language. In a recent correspondence with Rabbi Hoffman, he told me about a paper written by one of his rabbinical school students. The student, Joshua Franklin, reported that young Jews identify (tacitly) power words and problem words. Power words include vision, community, change, relationship, volunteer, grass roots, leadership, partnership, authentic, mission, empowerment, trust, transformation, spirituality, and tradition. Problem words include ethnicity, race, martyr, Holocaust, survival, creed, dogma, Temple, program, brotherhood, and frontal. Since this came after I had already finished my interviews, I decided to go back to the eight interviewees and test their reaction to these words.

Wondering if these words would track similarly with my mostly 40 to 65 response pool, I created a simple survey asking each interviewee to rank their reaction to each of the twenty-six words (see Appendix II). The words were listed randomly, mixing up power words with the problem words. It is important to note here that the sample size was too small to be considered scientific. If the sample size was larger, I would have removed the top and bottom extremes and used averages. With that said, the results are still interesting. Here are the results listed in order of the way the survey listed the words (the higher the score, the more positive the reaction) and distinguishing whether they are power or problem words:

1) Vision, 7.75, power

2) Community, 8.63, power

3) Ethnicity, 6.13, problem

4) Change, 6.25, power

5) Relationship, 7.00, power

6) Race, 5.00, problem

7) Martyr, 2.63, problem

8) Volunteer, 8.13, power

9) Grass roots, 6.88, power

[77] Ibid, 14.

10) Holocaust, 5.25, problem

11) Leadership, 8.50, power

12) Survival, 6.00, problem

13) Partnership, 7.00, power

14) Creed, 5.13, problem

15) Dogma, 3.88, problem

16) Authentic, 6.88, power

17) Mission, 7.13, power

18) Temple, 5.75, problem

19) Trust, 8.13, power

20) Program, 5.88, problem

21) Transformation, 6.50, power

22) Brotherhood, 5.75, problem

23) Frontal, 5.63, problem

24) Spirituality, 7.00, power

25) Tradition, 7.00, power

26) Empowerment, 7.13, power

Mr. Franklin may be on to something here. Taking the averages, power words score 6.87, problem words 5.18. This only confirms Franklin's assertion that the words have similar reactions from a larger pool of respondents and that they seem universal to age. Several stand out as important.

Community – 8.63. We know this follows general trends (or at least the stated desires) that Americans seek community. The phenomenon of social networking is one piece of evidence that people want to create communities based on a wide range of interests and affinities.

Relationship – 7.00. Jews want relationships first, affiliation second. The Next *Dor* project of Synagogue 3000 and accompanying research confirms this trend. The research, again by Cohen and Hoffman, reported, "Between the fall of 2009 and the summer of 2010, Synagogue 3000's Next *Dor* initiative inaugurated four experiments in engaging congregationally unaffiliated adult Jews in their 20s and 30s. They were set in widely scattered locations across the United States (Washington, DC; St. Louis; Marin County, CA; and Miami Beach). All four adhered to the Next *Dor* philosophy of providing relational engagement rather than just a series of unrelated programs..."[78] With relational engagement as an immutable tenet, "Regardless of profile, between 2009 when they began and 2010 when this survey was taken, they all grew in significant Jewish ways... Potential participants were approached using one-on-one organizational ways of thinking. The field workers in all four sites took a genuine interest in the people they met, striking up relationships, and inviting participation personally. At the same time, members of specific circles of engagement had their own network of contacts, sometimes in adjacent circles farther out, whom they invited personally as well. Had the Next *Dor* Jewish offerings not been of the quality they were, and had the relationships not deepened as a result of quality time spent together, invitees would not have returned. But, return they did. The more they returned, the more positive time they spent Jewishly, and the more positive time they spent Jewishly, the more they widened their Jewish involvement, acquired still newer Jewish friends, learned of opportunities for Jewish engagement even outside of Next *Dor*, and then brought friends made there to Next *Dor* as an obvious next step."[79] While Next *Dor* is focused on young Jewish adults, it seems clear that this constituency is not unique.

People seek relationships. Many of the interviewees talked about relationships as a key to their community connection; relationships with their rabbi(s), with other synagogue members, with community members, and the Jewish community at large were key factors for all. For several, seeking and finding relationships with Jewish text, ancestry and history was vital. This latter group commented that access to text study and ancestry was by and large a solo experience or, at the least, needed proactive engagement on their part. This appears a glaring omission by the synagogue community, since who better to provide fully egalitarian access to Jewish learning than synagogues? While many if not most synagogues provide adult learning opportunities, most are programmatic and parochial, often for 'members only.' Many that are not synagogue-based have Jews and non-Jews studying text and theology led by lay practitioners. While better than nothing, these sessions, often in the guise of interfaith dialogue, are led by practitioners who are not experts, nor are most capable of offering clear, relevant, factual information. But, that they proliferate in almost every community illustrates a need not met. Jews want a relationship with Judaism, but not in the way that the Jewish community offers.

---

[78] Steven M. Cohen and Lawrence Hoffman, "Different Growth for Different Folks: The ND Pilot Sites in Action," S3K Report (April 2011), 1.
[79] Ibid, 6.

Leadership – 8.50. I'm not clear how to interpret this high number, but based on the interviews, many expressed dismay at poor rabbinic leadership in their congregations. It did not seem that the rabbis were poor leaders as much as untrained in leadership. Several also spoke of unpleasant experiences as part of synagogue lay leadership.

Program – 5.88. That this is a problem word is underscored in the low score given by the interviewees. Synagogue members are tired of being 'programmed' rather than engaged. It is an accepted practice in synagogues to be program focused. If attendance is poor, the default reaction is to find "better programs." These rarely bring any better attendance other than the same pool of stalwart attendees who come regardless.

Spirituality – 7.00. Frankly, I was surprised by this number. While I had hoped it would follow the young adult trend expressed by Franklin, I was not sure if this sample would affirm its importance. I think it is important to point out that most of those in this group were very uncomfortable talking about spirituality, God, transcendence, or anything that inferred such. Several lamented that they wished they were more spiritual or better understood things spiritual, but uncomfortable nonetheless. However, at least as a group, the word scored very high on the scale affirming at least an implicit understanding of the importance of things beyond the physical.

To be clear, when speaking of spirituality, I am referring to something that is predominantly Jewish. By this, I mean to distinguish Jewish spiritual practice from Buddhism, the neo-Kabbalah movement, some new age spirituality, and even yoga and other meditative practices. While there is certainly nothing wrong with these and there is nothing inherently non-Jewish about them, for the purposes of this research, they muddy the waters of distinction. By Jewish spiritual practice, I am including prayer, study, meditation, social justice work, and community service that have a distinct Jewish flavor. As Cohen and Hoffman articulated in their study of Jewish Spirituality, "...specifically Jewish experiences too: seeing Jerusalem; experiencing Jewish community; and visiting remnants of Jewish communities in Europe. Regardless of what term Jews use, the parallel with what Christians name as 'spiritual' suggests that the same universal experiences named by Jews can be considered spirituality among Jews; the specifically Jewish instances would be Jewish spirituality."[80] Admittedly, even these are "tainted" with secularity and other religious influence, but so is the nature of Judaism. That many if not all of

---

[80]   Steven M. Cohen and Lawrence Hoffman, "How Spiritual Are America's Jews? Narrowing the Spirituality Gap Between Jews and Other Americans," S3K Report (March 2009), 4.

the interviewees named these experiences as important in their Jewish lives underscores the importance. That those who named experiences like visiting Eastern Europe as important but did not think of them as spiritual until asked again underscores a need for emphasis on those things and experiences that are uniquely, Jewishly spiritual. It is in these things that we will find Jewish people-hood, Jewishness as Hoffman contends, and perhaps the Jewish equivalent to Ecclesiology.

In order to further this conversation and create a public story about synagogues, they must be willing to experiment with charged words in the public domain. They must have conversations that use words like "spirituality", "God", and "meaning" in ways that outsiders can understand and participate. It may be that outsiders still do not become insiders. But, at least doing so will be the result of explicit reasons rather than tacit. I believe that many outsiders remain so because of their own ethnic sensibilities and experience. My belief, though, is that some will realize their own adamant beliefs are neither their own nor worth keeping when they see the value of being part of the Jewish community.

EVALUATION

As stated, success is subjective and my findings are open to interpretation. The next question is the viability and usefulness of the method. How might a congregation use this method and resulting information as a practical tool?

To be sure, interviews are time consuming. CTA as an interview method is even more time intensive since it requires at least a degree of methodology learning and familiarization. I do not think a congregational rabbi, for instance, would need to participate in intensive training about CTA. However, he or she would need an understanding of the approach, particularly its dynamic, fluid nature. Most importantly, CTA interviewing requires the interviewer to be a perceptive and observant listener. Without sharp listening skills, the interviews become simple, scripted question and answer conversations. It is in the ability to tenaciously dig down past the "why", beyond the "just because" or "I don't know" answers that reveal useful information for synagogue leaders.

And, then what is that information and what is its value? In this respect, synagogue leaders must be careful. Several, dare I say most, of the interviewees commented to me after our session that these questions were either things they had never thought of or thought about, and were reticent to address, since they did not want to think about the logical consequences of their answers. One interviewee shared with me several weeks afterward that our conversation was "really messing" with his synagogue membership and sense of Judaism. He also shared that he was thinking about spirituality (something he shared in the interview as an unattainable goal for him) in a very different way. This kind of inner reflection would be great for a sensitive, action-oriented synagogue leader who was also aware that building relationships with congregants was paramount to synagogue strength. It would also take a synagogue leader willing to hear things he or she might not want to hear. There was a good deal of criticism in the interviews. I am fairly certain that few of the leaders of these respective synagogues have heard these criticisms, at least in this brutally honest way.

As with other relational tools, CTA interviews are time intensive. They take preparation – gathering data (my survey), interpreting the data as it relates to each person, selecting interviewees, having the actual interview, transcribing and interpreting the interview information, and looking for patterns and cues. A synagogue leader need not conduct his or her research as an academic pursuit, but usable, reliable outcomes need a degree of rigor not usually carved out of a typical rabbi's schedule.

I believe it is worth the time and effort. Few methods offer or allow insight into the minds of congregants. Much of the information that surfaced in the interviews was ideas, beliefs, and values of which the interviewees were unaware. Several shared that sometimes they were actually surprised by their own answers. Yet, it is these tacit beliefs that inform much of what we do. In some cases, particularly when interviewees realized their tacit beliefs were not their own but some vestiges of ethnic nostalgia, interviewees allowed themselves to think more broadly and openly about their beliefs. I would imagine that for some, they might be challenging inherited beliefs from parents and grandparents and, possibly for the first time, deciding if these are, in fact, their own. This awareness might be the starting point for renewed commitment transforming synagogues and by extension, American Judaism.

BIBLIOGRAPHY

Ament, Jonathan. "American Jewish Religious Denominations." *United Jewish Communities*. Storrs, Connecticut: Center for Judaic Studies and Contemporary Jewish Life University of Connecticut, 2005. Print.

Borowitz, Eugene B. *Choices In Modern Jewish Thought: A Partisan Guide.* Springfield, New Jersey: Behrman House, 1995: 17. Print.

_____."Reform Judaism's Fresh Awareness of Religious Problems: Theological Conference-Cincinnati 1950." *Commentary* (June 1950): 571. Print.

Cohen, Steven M., and Lawrence Hoffman. "Different Growth for Different Folks: The ND Pilot Sites in Action." *S3K Reports* (April 2011): 1. Print.

Cohen, Steven M., and Lawrence Hoffman. "How Spiritual Are America's Jews." *S3K Reports* (March 2009): 14. Print.

Cohen, Steven M. "Members and Motives: Who Joins American Jewish Congregations and Why." *S3K Reports* (Fall 2006): 6. Print.

Conger, George. "Poll: US Jews Uninterested in Shul." *The Jerusalem Post, 20 April 2006.* Accessed 1 March 2009. http://www.jpost.com/LandedPages/PrintArticle.aspx?id=19401. Web.

Crandall, Beth, Gary Klein, and Robert Hoffman. *Working Minds: A Practitioner's Guide to Cognitive Task Analysis.* London: The MIT Press, 2006: 3. Print.

Elazar, Daniel J., and Stuart A. Cohen. *The Jewish Polity: Jewish Political Organization From Biblical Times to the Present.* Bloomington, Indiana: Indiana University Press, 1985: 13-15. Print.

Gladwell, Malcolm. *Blink: The Power of Thinking Without Thinking.* New York: Little, Brown and Company, 2005: 23. Print.

Goldy, Robert G. *The Emergence of Jewish Theology in America.* Bloomington, Indiana: Indiana University Press, 1990: 3, 13. Print.

Hoffman, Rabbi Lawrence. *ReThinking Synagogues: A New Vocabulary for Congregational Life.* Woodstock, Vermont: Jewish Lights, 2006: 6. Print.

Hoffman, Rabbi Lawrence A. *The Journey Home: Discovering the Deep Spiritual Wisdom of the Jewish Tradition.* Boston: Beacon Press, 2002: 69. Print.

Kelman, Ari, and Eliana Schonberg. *Legwork, Framework, Artwork: Engaging the Next Generation of Jews.* Denver, Colorado: The Rose Community Foundation, 2008. Print.

Klein Associates (Danyele Harris-Thompson and Sterling Wiggins). "Getting the Story Behind the Story: Putting Cognitive Task Analysis to Work." Indianapolis Center for Congregations, Indianapolis, Indiana, January 2005. Public Presentation.

Klein, Gary. *Sources of Power: How People Make Decisions.* London: The MIT Press, 1998: 4. Print.

Pines, Shlomo, translator. *Moses Maimonides: The Guide Of The Perplexed.* Chicago: The University of Chicago Press, 1963: 1-9. Print.

"Project Implicit." *Project Implicit.* IAT, Inc., n.d. Accessed 16 December 2011. https://implicit.harvard.edu/implicit/backgroundinformation.html. Web.

Swinton, John, and Harriett Mowat. *Practical Theology and Qualitative Research.* London: SCM Press, 2007: 29. Print.

Synagogue 3000. "Reform and Conservative Congregations: Different Strengths, Different Challenges." *S3K Reports* (March 2012): 2. Print.

Additional Resources

Ammerman, Nancy T., et al., ed. *Studying Congregations: A New Handbook.* Nashville, Tennessee: Abingdon Press, 1998. Print.

Aron, Isa. *A Congregation of Learners: Transforming the Synagogue into a Learning Community.* URJ Press, 1995. Print.

_____. *Becoming a Congregation of Learners: Learning As a Key to Revitalizing Congregational Life.* Woodstock, Vermont: Jewish Lights Publishing, 2000. Print.

Borowitz, Eugene B. *Studies In the Meaning of Judaism.* Philadelphia, PA: The Jewish Publication Society, 2002. Print.

_____. *Renewing the Covenant: A Theology for the Postmodern Jew.* Philadelphia, PA: The Jewish Publication Society, 1991. Print.

_____. Sigmund L. Falk Distinguished Professor of Education and Jewish Religious Thought at the New York School of Hebrew Union College - Jewish Institute of Religion. Email interview. 22 November 2005.

Butler-Bass, Diana. *The Practicing Congregation: Imagining a New Old Church.* Bethesda, Maryland: The Alban Institute, 2004. Print.

Cahalan, Kathleen A. *Projects That Matter: Successful Planning and Evaluation for Religious Organizations.* Bethesda, Maryland: Alban Institute, 1989. Print.

Chaves, Marc. *Congregations in America.* Cambridge, Massachusetts: Harvard University Press, 2004. Print.

Cohen, Steven M. "Engaging the Next Generation of American Jews: Distinguishing the In-married, Inter-married and Non-married." Draft copy prepared for *Journal of Jewish Communal Service* and the World Conference of Jewish Communal Service (Jerusalem: June 2006). Print.

Eliade, Mircea. *The Sacred and the Profane.* New York: Harcourt Brace, 1959. Print.

Friedman, Edwin. *A Failure Of Nerve: Leadership in the Age of the Quick Fix.* Bethesda, Maryland: Edwin Friedman Estate/Trust, 1999. Print.

Gilman, Neil. *Sacred Fragments: Recovering Theology for the Modern Jew.* Philadelphia, PA: The Jewish Publication Society, 1992. Print.

Heifetz, Ronald A. *Leadership Without Easy Answers.* Cambridge, Massachusetts: Harvard University Press, 1994. Print.

Heilman, Samuel C. *Synagogue Life: a Study in Symbolic Interaction.* Chicago: University of Chicago, 1976. Print.

Heller, Zachary I., ed. *Re-Envisioning The Synagogue.* Hollis, New Hampshire: Hollis Publishing Co., 2005. Print.

Hopewell, James F. *Congregation: Stories and Structures.* Philadelphia, PA: Fortress, 1987. Print.

Kaplan, Mordecai M. *Judaism As A Civilization: Toward a Reconstruction of American-Jewish Life.* Philadelphia, PA: Reconstructionist Press, 1981. Print.

————. *The Meaning of God in Modern Jewish Religion.* New York, NY: The Jewish Reconstructionist Foundation, 1947. Print.

Michaelson, Jay. "A Prayer Group of Their Own." *The Forward,* 14 November 2003. Print.

Morgan, Michael L. *Interim Judaism: Jewish Thought in a Century of Crisis.* Bloomington, IN: Indiana University Press, 2001. Print.

Novak, David. *Talking With Christians: Musings of A Jewish Theologian.* Grand Rapids, MI: Wm. B. Eerdmans Publishing Company, 2005. Print.

Price Brown, Sarah. "Emergent Jews Worshippers create unconventional communities unbound by tradition to reinvigorate Judaism." *The Jewish Journal of Greater Los Angeles,* 27 January 2006. Print.

Schwarz, Sidney. *Finding a Spiritual Home: How a New Generation of Jews Can Transform the American Synagogue.* Woodstock, Vermont: Jewish Lights Publishing, 2003. Print.

Sonsino, Rifat, and Daniel B. Syme. *Finding God: Ten Jewish Responses.* New York, NY:

Union of American Hebrew Congregations Press, 1986. Print.

Silverstein, Alan. *Alternatives to Assimilation: The Response of Reform Judaism to American Culture 1840-1930.* Boston, MA: Brandeis Press, 1994. Print.

Wertheimer, Jack, ed. *The American Synagogue.* Hanover, NH: Brandeis University Press, 1987. Print.

Wyschogrod, Michael, and R. Kendall Soulen. *Abraham's Promise: Judaism and Jewish-Christian Relations.* Grand Rapids, MI: Wm. B. Eerdmans Publishing Company, 2004. Print.

APPENDICES

APPENDIX I – ORIGINAL SURVEY

1. Introduction

The following survey is part one of my doctoral project research. I greatly appreciate your taking the time to answer the following questions. It shouldn't take more than 15 minutes. This data will give me a baseline for my research. It will be held in strict confidence and no personal information will be shared.

I contend, and other research shows, that Jewish identity in America can no longer rely on culture or ethnicity to sustain it, as it has in previous generations. Affiliation rates in synagogues (and generally in the Jewish community) are on a steady decline and American Jews, particularly younger Jews, see little value in affiliation. The American Jewish community is more intimate and comfortable with the non-Jewish world than ever in history. This intimacy has enabled Jews to thrive as never before. This comfort is countered by a downside – with acceptance by its non-Jewish neighbors comes new levels of acculturation – Jews want to be like their non-Jewish contemporaries. The American Jewish community wrestles with the fine line between acculturation and distinctive Jewishness. This then leads to the question, why be Jewish?

Past motivations including ethnic identifications no longer sustain the Jewish community. Without these ethnic and even cultural distinctions, the Jewish community is seeking something else that creates uniqueness and connectedness. It is my contention, that the "something else" is a reclaiming of our collective wisdom of lived theology (Jewishness) especially as it pertains to synagogues.

I believe this collective wisdom lies somewhere in the tacit knowledge of many synagogue members. If I simply ask, "Why are you a member of a synagogue?" the answers are varied but include some version of "I'm not sure." Through an interview process called cognitive task analysis (CTA) and cognitive decision making (CDM) I hope to tease out the unknown. This survey is the first step of that process.

If you have any questions feel free to contact me. Thank you!

Rabbi Aaron Spiegel
aspiegel@centerforcongregations.org
317-418-5488.

2. About you...

1. Your information: (please note, while optional, this information is very important for follow up and evaluation purposes)

Name:

Company:

Address:

Address 2:

City/Town:

State:

ZIP:

Country:

Email Address:

Phone Number:

2. Age group

◯ 18 - 25

◯ 26 - 39

◯ 40 - 65

◯ 65 and over

3. I'm affiliated with a synagogue (dues paying member)

◯ Yes

◯ No

4. Synagogue name (if affiliated with more than one synagogue please list the primary congregation or the one you feel most connected)

5. I consider myself

◯ Reform

◯ Conservative

◯ Orthodox

◯ Reconstructionist

◯ Just Jewish

Other (please specify)

6. Comments for this page:

6. If yes, that experience was...

○ Life affirming

○ Positive

○ Mostly good

○ Neutral

○ Not good

○ Negative

○ Terrible

Comments

[ ]

7. If married (or married in the past), was the wedding in a synagogue?

○ Yes

○ No

8. I'm at the synagogue for ...

	Less than once a month	At least once a quarter	Once a month	More than once a month	Weekly when possible
Worship (regardless whether there's a bar/bat mitzvah)	○	○	○	○	○
Other business	○	○	○	○	○

9. Comments for this page:

[ ]

1. Are you a member of a JCC?

○ Yes

○ No

2. Have you been to Israel?

○ Yes

○ No

3. Synagogue membership is important...

not really	a little	important	very important	essential
○	○	○	○	○

4. To what extent do you agree or disagree with the following statements?

	Strongly Disagree	Disagree	Mixed, not sure	Agree	Strongly Agree
I feel knowledgeable about Jewish life	○	○	○	○	○
Being Jewish adds meaning to my life	○	○	○	○	○
I have a strong sense of belonging to the Jewish people	○	○	○	○	○
It's important to me to have many friends who are Jewish	○	○	○	○	○
Hardly any of my friends are into being Jewish in a big way	○	○	○	○	○
Judaism doesn't say much to me about things that are really important to me	○	○	○	○	○
Synagogue membership is essential to my Jewishness	○	○	○	○	○
I socialize mostly with other members of my synagogue	○	○	○	○	○

5. Have you ever held a position of leadership in a synagogue (board member, religious school teacher, project leader, gabbai, worship leader, Torah reader, etc).

○ Yes

○ No

109

4. Jewish education...

1. I attended or participated in (check all that apply)

☐ Jewish day school

☐ Jewish high school

☐ Sunday school

☐ Hebrew school

2. I attended a Jewish camp

○ Yes

○ No

3. I am or was a member of a Jewish youth group (NFTY, USY, BBYO, NCSY, etc)

○ Yes

○ No

4. I am or was active in Hillel

○ Yes

○ No

5. Comments for this page:

110

5. Family history...

1. In terms of my religious upbringing, I was raised

- ○ Jewish
- ○ Jewish and something else
- ○ Not Jewish

It's complicated (please explain)

[   ]

2. My father is Jewish

- ○ Yes
- ○ No

3. If yes, he considers himself

- ○ Reform
- ○ Conservative
- ○ Orthodox
- ○ Reconstructionist
- ○ Just Jewish

Other (please specify) or not applicable

[   ]

4. My mother is Jewish

- ○ Yes
- ○ No

5. If yes, she considers herself

- ○ Reform
- ○ Conservative
- ○ Orthodox
- ○ Reconstructionist
- ○ Just Jewish

Other (please specify) or not applicable

[   ]

6. As a child, my family was a member of a synagogue?

○ Yes

○ No

7. Our family considered itself

○ Reform

○ Conservative

○ Orthodox

○ Reconstructionist

○ Just Jewish

Other (please specify) or not applicable

[_____]

8. My siblings

number of brothers [_____]

number of sisters [_____]

Sibling #1

9. Is Jewish

○ Yes

○ No

10. Is a member of a synagogue

○ Yes

○ No

Sibling #2

11. Is Jewish

○ Yes

○ No

12. Is a member of a synagogue

○ Yes

○ No

Sibling #3

13. Is Jewish

○ Yes

○ No

14. Is a member of a synagogue

⭕ Yes

⭕ No

Sibling #4

15. Is Jewish

⭕ Yes

⭕ No

16. Is a member of a synagogue

⭕ Yes

⭕ No

17. Comments for this page:

APPENDIX II – POWER WORDS SURVEY

Please rank your immediate response to the following words or phrases with 0 being most negative and 10 being most positive.

1. vision

very negative   neutral   very positive

O   O   O   O   O   O   O   O   O   O

2. community

very negative   neutral   very positive

O   O   O   O   O   O   O   O   O   O

3. ethnicity

very negative   neutral   very positive

O   O   O   O   O   O   O   O   O   O

4. change

very negative   neutral   very positive

O   O   O   O   O   O   O   O   O   O

5. relationship

very negative   neutral   very positive

O   O   O   O   O   O   O   O   O   O

6. race

very negative   neutral   very positive

O   O   O   O   O   O   O   O   O   O

7. martyr

very negative   neutral   very positive

O   O   O   O   O   O   O   O   O   O

8. volunteer

very negative   neutral   very positive

O   O   O   O   O   O   O   O   O   O

9. grass roots

very negative   neutral   very positive

O   O   O   O   O   O   O   O   O   O

10. holocaust

very negative   neutral   very positive

O   O   O   O   O   O   O   O   O   O

11. leadership

very negative   neutral   very positive

O   O   O   O   O   O   O   O   O   O

12. survival

very negative   neutral   very positive

O   O   O   O   O   O   O   O   O   O

13. partnership

very negative   neutral   very positive

O   O   O   O   O   O   O   O   O   O

14. creed

very negative   neutral   very positive

O   O   O   O   O   O   O   O   O   O

15. dogma

very negative   neutral   very positive

O   O   O   O   O   O   O   O   O   O

16. authentic

very negative   neutral   very positive

O   O   O   O   O   O   O   O   O   O

17. mission

very negative   neutral   very positive

O   O   O   O   O   O   O   O   O   O

18. temple

very negative   neutral   very positive

O   O   O   O   O   O   O   O   O   O

19. trust

very negative   neutral   very positive

O   O   O   O   O   O   O   O   O   O

20. program

very negative   neutral   very positive

O   O   O   O   O   O   O   O   O   O

21. transformation

very negative   neutral   very positive

O   O   O   O   O   O   O   O   O   O

22. brotherhood

very negative   neutral   very positive

O   O   O   O   O   O   O   O   O   O

23. frontal

very negative   neutral   very positive

O   O   O   O   O   O   O   O   O   O

24. spirituality

very negative   neutral   very positive

O   O   O   O   O   O   O   O   O   O

25. tradition

very negative   neutral   very positive

O   O   O   O   O   O   O   O   O   O

26. empowerment

very negative   neutral   very positive

O   O   O   O   O   O   O   O   O   O

Made in the USA
San Bernardino, CA
20 June 2017